CRYPTO BULLION
HISTORY OF THE FIRST YEAR

A DECENTRALISED CRYPTOCURRENCY
PART OF THE "ALT-ERNATIVE" BOOK SERIES

Crypto Bullion—History of the First Year
by Christopher P. Thompson

Copyright © 2016 by Christopher P. Thompson

All rights reserved.

Book Author by Christopher P. Thompson

Book Design by C. Ellis

No part of this book may be reproduced in any written, electronic, recording, or photocopying without written permission of the publisher or author. The exception would be in the case of brief quotations embodied in the critical articles or reviews, images and pages where permission is specifically granted by the publisher or author.

Although every precaution has been taken to verify the accuracy of the information contained herein, the author and publisher assume no responsibility for any errors or omissions. No liability is assumed for damages that may result from the use of information contained within.

ISBN—13: 978-1537636023
ISBN—10: 1537636022

CRYPTO BULLION
HISTORY OF THE FIRST YEAR

A DECENTRALISED CRYPTOCURRENCY
PART OF THE "ALT-ERNATIVE" BOOK SERIES

CHRISTOPHER P. THOMPSON

ABOUT THE AUTHOR

Christopher Paul Thompson is an avid cryptocurrency enthusiast from the United Kingdom. Born in Bradford, UK and academically educated at the University of York (BSc Mathematics). He has been a keen follower of past and current events in the crypto space since March 2013. His first book called Cryptocurrency "The Alt-ernative" A Beginner's Reference is the first book he has ever written.

Other titles currently available:

"Peercoin—History of the First Year"
"Reddcoin—History of the First Year"
"DigiByte—History of the First Year"
"Dogecoin—History of the First Year"
"GoldCoin—History of the First Year"
"Digitalcoin—History of the First Year"

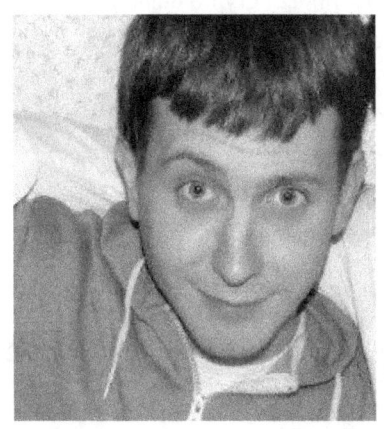

Other titles to be released soon:

"Trumpcoin—Make Crypto Great Again"
"Anoncoin—History of the First Year"
"Yocoin—History of the First Year"
"Diamond—An Extended History"
"Mooncoin—Philosophy of Decentralisation"
"Unobtanium—An Extended History"

E-mail Contact: chris_thompson25@live.co.uk
Twitter Contact: https://twitter.com/MrSilverCider

Crypto Bullion—History of the First Year

CONTENTS

Introduction	10-11
What is Crypto Bullion?	12
Why use Crypto Bullion?	13
Is Crypto Bullion Money?	14
Crypto Bullion Specification	15
Crypto Bullion Milestone Timeline	16-19
Crypto Bullion Blockchain	20-21
Proof of Work (PoW) Mining	22
Block Time of Crypto Bullion	23
Block Reward Distribution Table	24
Crypto Bullion Wallets	25
First Year Crypto Bullion Exchanges	26
Current Crypto Bullion Exchanges	27
Crypto Bullion Team	28-29
Crypto Bullion Community	30
First Year History of Crypto Bullion	31
The Launch of the Crypto Bullion Blockchain (JUNE 2013)	32-37
First Two Cryptocurrency Exchanges Initiated CBX Trading (JULY 2013)	38-45
New Coin Logo Unveiled and Official Website Launched (AUGUST 2013)	47-53
Market Capitalisation Began to Surge (SEPTEMBER 2013)	55-61

CONTENTS

New Official Block Explorer Launched (OCTOBER 2013)	....	63-69
FiniteByDesign One Ounce .999 Silver Bars Made Available (NOVEMBER 2013)	....	71-77
All Time High Market Capitalisation of Crypto Bullion Attained (DECEMBER 2013)	....	79-83
New Plans for Crypto Bullion in 2014 (JANUARY 2014)	....	85-91
Director of Marketing and Strategy User "papersheepdog" Joined the CBX Team (FEBRUARY 2014)	....	93-99
Lead Developer Resigned and Four Exchanges Initiated CBX Trading (MARCH 2014)	....	101-107
Direct Fiat to CBX Trading Made Available By Vault of Satoshi (APRIL 2014)	....	109-113
CryptoTown On The Ground Project (MAY 2014)	....	115-117
One Year Anniversary of Crypto Bullion (JUNE 2014)	....	119-123
APPENDIX	....	125
Article One (10th of September 2013)	....	127-129
Article Two (18th of November 2013)	....	131-133

INTRODUCTION

Cryptocurrency was born with the advent of Bitcoin. It was first mentioned in a research paper published online titled "Bitcoin: A Peer-to-Peer Electronic Cash System" with the real name or pseudonym Satoshi Nakamoto attributed to it. This paper was published on the 31st of October 2008. About two months later on the 3rd of January 2009, the Bitcoin network protocol was launched. This technological breakthrough was the beginning of a decentralized public ledger. It allows people to send value across the globe without the permission of a third party authority.

Since then, a growing number of people around the world have been introduced to or discovered cryptocurrency. Many cryptocurrencies have been launched over the following years since the introduction of Bitcoin. The name "alternative" was given to these cryptocurrencies after Bitcoin because they were developed, implemented and introduced to be used instead of or alongside Bitcoin. One could say, a choice of brand in cryptocurrency exists. People have discovered these either through word of mouth, by accident, through personal investigation or via the media. Nevertheless, it has changed the lives of many people. It has provoked the general public into asking innumerable questions about many issues based on subjects such as economics, politics, philosophy, mathematics and so on.

In this book, I hope to give the reader insight into how one particular alternative cryptocurrency began. Crypto Bullion began in 2013 as a Scrypt proof of work/proof of stake clone of Novacoin which, in turn, was derived from Peercoin. This book, as well as other future books to be written on other cryptocurrencies, is a historical story of the first year. It covers the time from the initial announcement on Bitcointalk up until the blockchain had been publicly available for one year. In this case, from the 27th of June 2013 to the 28th of June 2014. It also describes the terminology one encounters in cryptocurrency such as proof of work mining, block reward, wallets and so on.

INTRODUCTION

I chose to write about just the first year for various reasons, some of which are:

- For almost all cryptocurrencies, the first year of their existence is the most defining period.
- If I had chosen to write a full history of Crypto Bullion, I would be continuously playing catch up.
- Currently I have a full-time job besides being a cryptocurrency author, so my time is unfortunately limited.

Crypto Bullion was originally known as Cryptogenic Bullion throughout the first year of its existence. It is evident in the personal quotes that this was the case. Nevertheless, I refer to the coin as Crypto Bullion in this book. The name change occurred in 2015.

You may have bought this book because Crypto Bullion is your favourite cryptocurrency. Alternatively, you may be keen to find out how it all began. I have presented the information henceforth without going into too much technical discussion about Crypto Bullion. If you would like to investigate further, I recommend that you read material currently available online at the official website at http://cryptobullion.io/.

If you choose to purchase a certain amount of Crypto Bullion, please do not buy more than you can afford to lose.

Enjoy the book :D

WHAT IS CRYPTO BULLION?

Crypto Bullion is a cryptocurrency or digital decentralised currency/commodity used via the Internet. It is described as a payment network without the need for a central authority such as a bank or other central clearing house. It allows the end user to store or transfer value anywhere in the world with the use of a personal computer, laptop or smartphone. Cryptography has been implemented and coded into the network allowing the user to send currency through a decentralised (no centre point of failure), open source (anyone can review the code), peer-to-peer network. Cryptography also controls the creation of newly minted units of CBX account.

The Crypto Bullion network protocol was created by using the source code inherent in the Scrypt based coin called Novacoin. The developers of Crypto Bullion altered the code to produce an alternative coin with a differing block reward schedule, block time, difficulty re-targeting time and projected number of coins.

On the official website, the description of Crypto Bullion is:

"Released in late June 2013, Crypto Bullion was designed primarily for the purpose of storing wealth. Crypto Bullion is a second generation crypto-currency designed to emulate the properties and supply of gold. It's the first crypto-currency to display all of the properties of money, while providing the bearer with interest for holding it. Crypto Bullion is also the first to employ its pioneering Proof-of-Stake-Participation (PoSP) algorithm which has taken the strength of traditional proof-of-stake implementations, extreme energy efficiency, and injected revolutionary designs to configure the algorithm for maximum security and function."

The slogan used by the Crypto Bullion community to market the coin is:

"THE DIGITAL PRECIOUS METAL"

WHY USE CRYPTO BULLION?

Like all cryptocurrencies, people have chosen to adopt Crypto Bullion as a medium of exchange or store of wealth through personal choice. An innovative feature of the coin, an affinity towards the brand or high confidence of the community could be reasons why they have done so. Key benefits of using Crypto Bullion are:

- It is a useful medium of exchange via which value can be transferred internationally for a fraction of the cost of other conventional methods.
- Crypto Bullion eliminates the need for a trusted third party such as a bank, clearing house or other centralised authority (e.g. PayPal). All transactions are solely from one person to another (peer-to-peer).
- Crypto Bullion has the potential to engage people worldwide who are without a bank account (unbanked).
- Crypto Bullion is immune from the effects of hyperinflation, unlike the current fiat monetary systems around the world.

The most defining characteristic of the coin, as was initially stated by the developers, is its relatively small coin circulation. Approximately one million CBX have been mined or staked since its launch in June 2013. This is less than 5% of the total cap of all Bitcoins to be mined. As a result, Crypto Bullion is described fundamentally as a rare, precious and scarce crypto commodity intended to keep its value as a store of wealth. Since the vast majority of CBX were mined via proof of work, there has been an annual inflation of 1-2 %. This increase of the coin circulation comes from wallet client users earning CBX on their holdings. After a certain time period, coins are deposited into that user's wallet.

IS CRYPTO BULLION MONEY?

Money is a form of acceptable, convenient and valued medium of payment for goods and services within an economy. It allows two parties to exchange goods or services without the need to barter. This eradicates the potential situation where one party of the two may not want what the other has to offer. The main properties of money are:

- **As a medium of exchange**—money can be used as a means to buy/sell goods/services without the need to barter.

- **A unit of account**—a common measure of value wherever one is in the world.

- **Portable**—easily transferred from one party to another. The medium used can be easily carried.

- **Durable**—all units of the currency can be lost, but not destroyed.

- **Divisible**—each unit can be subdivided into smaller fractions of that unit.

- **Fungible**— each unit of account is the same as every other unit within the medium (1 CBX = 1 CBX)

- **As a store of value**—it sustains its purchasing power (what it can buy) over long periods of time.

Crypto Bullion easily satisfies the first six characteristics. Taking into account the last characteristic, the value of Crypto Bullion, like all currencies, comes from people willing to accept it as a medium of exchange for payment of goods or services. As it gets adopted by more individuals or merchants, its intrinsic value will increase accordingly.

CRYPTO BULLION SPECIFICATION

Since the birth of Crypto Bullion, its coin specification has changed a few times. At the time of publication of this book, its current specification is:

Coin Symbol:	CBX (originally known as CGB)
Unit of account:	CBX (originally known as CGB)
Date of Announcement:	28th of June 2013 at 01:22:13 UTC
Genesis Block Generated:	27th of June 2013 at 16:52:05 UTC
Block Number One Generated:	27th of June 2013 at 17:46:02 UTC
Date of Launch:	28th of June 2013
Founder:	user "elambert"
Lead Developer:	user "Alex4J"
Hashing Algorithms:	Scrypt
Timestamping Algorithm:	Proof of Stake Participation (PoSP)
Address Begins With:	5
Total Coins:	1 million (1-2% annual inflation)
Block Time:	65 seconds
Difficulty Retarget Time:	65 seconds
Coins per Block:	(see page 24)
Confirmations per Transaction:	5
Pre-mine:	9,339.899 CBX

CRYPTO BULLION MILESTONE TIMELINE

27th of June 2013	—Block number one timestamped at 17:46:02 UTC.
28th of June 2013	—Bitcointalk forum thread created at 01:22:13 UTC
28th of June 2013	—Pre-mine of 9,339.88 CGB mined at 01:53:32 UTC.
28th of June 2013	—First block explorer created by user "diatonic".
1st of July 2013	—Exchange Coins-e initiated live trading of CBX.
12th of July 2013	—New wallet client update released.
25th of July 2013	—Exchange Cryptsy initiated live trading of CBX.
30th of July 2013	—New wallet client update released.
31st of July 2013	—Block reward did not halve at block number 50,001.
1st of August 2013	—New wallet client update released.
4th of August 2013	—Reward per proof of work block halved for the first time from 10 CBX to 5 CBX.
4th of August 2013	—CBX added to www.coinmarketcap.com.
5th of August 2013	—New wallet client update released.
7th of August 2013	—Exchange CoinEx initiated live trading of CBX.
10th of August 2013	—Brand new CBX coin logo design published.
11th of August 2013	—http://cryptogenicbullion.org website launched.
16th of August 2013	—Version 1.1.5.3 wallet client released (optional).
18th of August 2013	—Chinese version of the official website launched.
1st of September 2013	—Reward per proof of work block halved for the second time from 5 CBX to 2.5 CBX.
4th of September 2013	—Exchange PhenixEx initiated live trading of CBX.
10th of September 2013	—Yahoo Finance article published.
19th of September 2013	—Surge in CBX Bitcoin Satoshi value.
27th of September 2013	—Version 1.1.6.3 wallet client released.

CRYPTO BULLION MILESTONE TIMELINE

6th of October 2013	—Blog section added to the official CBX website.
6th of October 2013	—Reward per proof of work block halved for the third time from 2.5 CBX to 1.25 CBX.
10th of October 2013	—One unit of CBX account surpassed $0.50.
13th of October 2013	—An exclusive CBX block explorer went live at http://explorer.cryptogenicbullion.org.
30th of October 2013	—Original CBX Subreddit was created at www.reddit.com/r/CryptogenicBullion.
5th of November 2013	—Version 1.1.6.4 Windows wallet client released.
6th of November 2013	—Version 1.1.6.4 Mac OS X wallet client released.
10th of November 2013	—Reward per proof of work block halved for the fourth time from 1.25 CBX to 0.625 CBX.
16th of November 2013	—Market capitalisation surpassed $1 million.
18th of November 2013	—Second Yahoo Finance article published.
30th of November 2013	—Physical one ounce .999 CBX silver bars available.
1st of December 2013	—All time high market capitalisation of ~$5,663,750 attained according to www.coinmarketcap.com.
14th of December 2013	—Cryptsy initiated direct CBX/LTC trading.
15th of December 2013	—Reward per proof of work block halved for the fifth time from 0.625 CBX to 0.3125 CBX.
19th of December 2013	—FiniteByDesign released Crypto Card Paper Wallets.
30th of December 2013	—One unit of CBX account was valued at ~$2.21.
31st of December 2013	—Block number 268,311 was the last block timestamped in 2013.

CRYPTO BULLION MILESTONE TIMELINE

7th of January 2014	—Version 1.1.6.5 of the Windows wallet client released.
8th of January 2014	—Version 1.1.6.5 of the Mac wallet client released.
9th of January 2014	—Exchange OpenEx initiated live trading of CBX.
16th of January 2014	—Winner of the "CB 2013 Partnership Award" announced as www.coinpayments.net.
19th of January 2014	—Reward per proof of work block halved for the sixth time from 0.3125 CBX to 0.15625 CBX.
1st of February 2014	—Exchange Cryptokopen initiated live trading of CBX.
3rd of February 2014	—First comment submitted by user "papersheepdog".
5th of February 2014	—Lighter version of the official website snubbed.
9th of February 2014	—Paper wallet generator at http://cgbaddress.org released thanks to user "x0rcist".
10th of February 2014	—First promotional video uploaded for CBX.
19th of February 2014	—CBX TipBot went live on Reddit.
20th of February 2014	—Gold themed CBX coin logo designs published.
23rd of February 2014	—Reward per proof of work block halved for the seventh time from 0.15625 CBX to 0.078125 CBX.
1st of March 2014	—User "mercSuey" resigned from the CBX Team.
1st of March 2014	—User "artiface" became the new lead developer.
4th of March 2014	—A new list of CBX Team members published.
8th of March 2014	—Version 1.1.6.6 of the wallet client released.
10th of March 2014	—Exchange AllCrypt initiated live trading of CBX.
19th of March 2014	—New official website at http://cgb.holdings went live.
23rd of March 2014	—Exchange Bittrex initiated live trading of CBX.
23rd of March 2014	—Prizes of the "Viral Image Contest" were announced.

CRYPTO BULLION MILESTONE TIMELINE

23rd of March 2014	—Exchange Ecoinfund initiated live trading of CBX.
28th of March 2014	—Exchange Swaphole initiated live trading of CBX.
30th of March 2014	—Reward per proof of work block halved for the eighth time from 0.078125 CBX to 0.039062 CBX.
5th of April 2014	—Exchange PTOPEX initiated live trading of CBX.
9th of April 2014	—Version 1.1.6.7 of the wallet client released.
10th of April 2014	—Exchange Vault of Satoshi initiated live trading of CBX.
21st of April 2014	—A contest called "News Beat" closed.
23rd of April 2014	—User "Matheltu1" joined the development team.
27th of April 2014	—Exchange Comkort initiated live trading of CBX.
28th of April 2014	—Winners of the "News Beat" contest revealed.
4th of May 2014	—Reward per proof of work block halved for the ninth time from 0.039062 CBX to 0.019531 CBX.
6th of May 2014	—Suggestions sought after about how to celebrate the first birthday of the coin.
26th of May 2014	—An project called "CryptoTown On The Ground" was announced by user "papersheepdog".
8th of June 2014	—No PoW block reward reduction occurred at block number 495,001.
18th of June 2014	—Discussion about the coin specification took place.
27th of June 2014	—Donations for a professional marketing campaign requested.
27th of June 2014	—the last block of the first year existence of the blockchain was timestamped at 17:43:32 UTC.
28th of June 2014	—the last block during which the blockchain had been publicly available was timestamped at 01:56:59 UTC.

CRYPTO BULLION BLOCKCHAIN

Every cryptocurrency has a corresponding blockchain within its decentralised network protocol. Crypto Bullion is no different in this sense. A blockchain is simply described as a general public ledger of all transactions and blocks ever executed since the very first block. In addition, it continuously updates in real time each time a new block is successfully mined/minted. Blocks enter the blockchain in such a manner that each block contains the hash of the previous one. It is therefore utterly resistant to modification along the chain since each block is related to the prior one. Consequently, the problem of doubling-spending is solved.

As a means for the general public to view the blockchain, web developers have created block explorers. The first block explorer for Crypto Bullion was made available at the domain http://cgb.webboise.com:2770 thanks to user "diatonic". It was announced as being accessible on the 28th of June 2013. However, it no longer exists.

Since the inception of the first block explorer, other websites have been created. Currently there is only one explorer for the coin at:

- https://chainz.cryptoid.info/cbx/;

On the 11th of September 2016 at 12:39 UTC, the Bitcoin Satoshi value of one CBX unit of account was 46,550 according to the above block explorer. This equated to an approximate US Dollar figure of $0.29, a market capitalisation of $284,796 and 982,064 CBX generated since the coin launched in June 2013.

CRYPTO BULLION BLOCKCHAIN

Block explorers tend to present different layouts, statistics and charts. Some are more extensive in terms of the information given. Some statistics include:

- **Height of block** —the block number of the network.
- **Time of block** —the time at which the block was timestamped to the blockchain.
- **Transactions** —the number of transactions in that particular block.
- **Total Sent** —the total amount of cryptocurrency sent in that particular block.
- **Block Reward** —how many coins were generated in the block (added to the overall coin circulation).

Below is a screenshot of block number one from the block explorer at https://chainz.cryptoid.info/cbx/:

Details for Block #1

Hash	00000c98ca5027576dcdf662cedd271db881f5fe6e781a220bdd08e11da1a094
Date/Time	2013-06-27 17:46:02
Transactions	1
Value Out	10.0 CBX
Difficulty	0.00024414
Outstanding	10.0 CBX
Created	10.0 CBX

Hash	Value Out	From (amount)	To (amount)	
ea2697630649...	10.0 CBX	Generation + Fees	5Z8BmjtqbOi6Q1WtbmtzxFmbhmwJXkYFCS	10.0 CBX

PROOF OF WORK (PoW) MINING

Proof of work mining is a competitive computerised process which helps to maintain and secure the blockchain in such a way as to verify transactions and prevent double spending.

In the general sense of cryptocurrency, those who participate in the activity of mining are called miners. They are general members of the cryptocurrency community who dedicate processing power (hash) of their computers towards solving highly complex mathematical problems and verifying transactions. This process upholds the integrity and security of the network. As such, miners are described as protectors of the network. Each transaction (held within a certain block) is validated before adding it to the blockchain. By doing this, they are rewarded (as an incentive) with newly generated mined coins or transaction fees. These coins are issued by the software in a transparent and predictable way outside of the control of its founders and developers. A miner can be based anywhere in the world as long as they have an internet connection, sufficient knowledge of how one mines and the hardware/software required to do so.

Miners use GPUs (Graphical Processing Units) or CPUs (Central Processing Units) to process transactions by hashing. Also, Application Specific Integrated Circuits (ASICs) allow miners to use customised hardware for faster and lower power mining.

When Crypto Bullion launched, the timestamping algorithm was hybrid proof of work/stake. This remained the case until the 1st of January 2016. Since then, the timestamping algorithm has been Proof of Stake Participation (an innovative form of proof of stake timestamping from the development team).

Proof of work mining was used to quickly generate the mass majority of CBX units of account from the 27th of June 2013 to the 13th of July 2014.

BLOCK TIME OF CRYPTO BULLION

The block time is the average time taken for the network to successfully generate a certain block either by proof of work or proof of stake. Both the reward and time of all blocks generated dictate how the circulation of coins grows over time.

Originally, the block time of the network protocol was pre-determined to permit miners to find one block every sixty seconds (on average). The first twelve blocks timestamped to the blockchain on the 27th of June 2013 were:

Block Number 1	17:46:02 UTC	Block Number 7	17:46:15 UTC
Block Number 2	17:46:04 UTC	Block Number 8	17:46:17 UTC
Block Number 3	17:46:06 UTC	Block Number 9	17:46:18 UTC
Block Number 4	17:46:09 UTC	Block Number 10	17:46:20 UTC
Block Number 5	17:46:12 UTC	Block Number 11	17:46:22 UTC
Block Number 6	17:46:13 UTC	Block Number 12	17:46:24 UTC

As is evident above, it took twenty two seconds to find the first twelve blocks. This was the result of low initial difficulty and very high processing power committed by the development team to the network protocol at the beginning. All 120 CBX generated in these twelve blocks went towards the pre-mine of the coin.

At present, the average block time of each proof of stake participation (PoSP) block timestamped to the blockchain is sixty five seconds.

BLOCK REWARD DISTRIBUTION TABLE

As time progresses, a certain number of coins (reward) are generated each time a block has been mined, verified and added to the blockchain. As is almost often the case, the reward per block decreases to a lower value at a pre-determined block number. This was the case for Crypto Bullion.

During the time when the timestamping algorithm was hybrid proof of work/stake, the proportion of proof of stake blocks grew from just below 10% at the end of 2013 to 70% in June 2014. At the present time, the timestamping algorithm is solely a form of proof of stake known as PoSP (Proof of Stake Participation).

On the 13th of July 2014, the block reward of each proof of work block reduced for the final time to 0.01 CBX. This began at block number 545,001.

On the first day of 2016, proof of work mining ceased to be possible. Via PoSP, 1-2% more CBX are added to the overall coin circulation on an annual basis.

What follows is the block reward distribution table from 2013/14:

Date of Initial Block	Initial Block	Last Block	Number of Blocks	Reward	Cumulative Total
27/06/2013	1	934	934 (pre-mine)	10	9,339.899
28/06/2013	935	55,000	54,066	10	545,405.74972101
04/08/2013	55,001	95,000	40,000	5	725,496.77366419
01/09/2013	95,001	145,000	50,000	2.5	838,803.04969819
06/10/2013	145,001	195,000	50,000	1.25	895,483.83496919
10/11/2013	195,001	245,000	50,000	0.625	921,438.55980619
15/12/2013	245,001	295,000	50,000	0.3125	936,126.87035819
19/01/2014	295,001	345,000	50,000	0.15625	943,559.12679919
23/02/2014	345,001	395,000	50,000	0.078125	947,708.61794119
30/03/2014	395,001	445,000	50,000	0.039062	950,034.32962019
04/05/2014	445,001	545,000	100,000	0.019531	952,961.63887619
13/07/2014	545,001			0.01	

CRYPTO BULLION WALLETS

A wallet is basically a piece of software that can be used on a personal computer, tablet or smartphone. It allows users to store Crypto Bullion as well as execute transfers of CBX with other users. Alternatively, it can be described as a means to access the coins from the inseparable blockchain (public transaction ledger). The wallet cryptographically generates and holds the public and private keys necessary to make these transactions possible. The software can be accessed, downloaded and installed from the official website by clicking on the "Downloads" option at the top that homepage:

- http://cryptobullion.io

Crypto Bullion wallets have been developed to work on the operating systems Windows, Mac OS X and Linux. Currently, there are several types of wallet available to the community. These are depicted as follows:

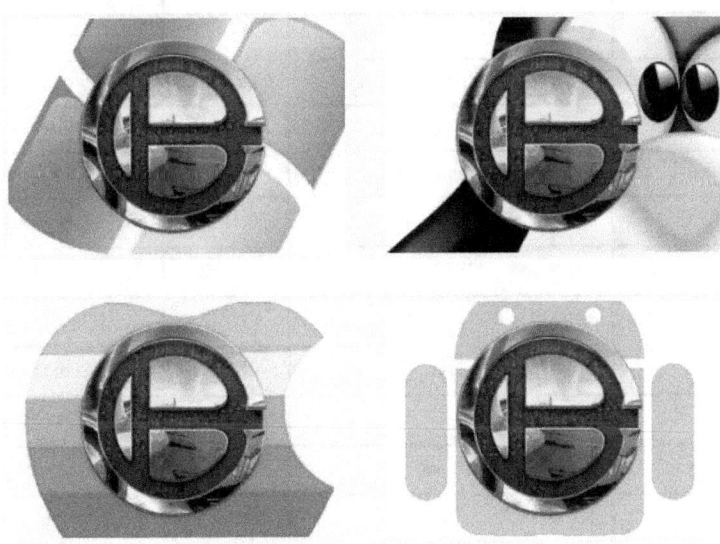

FIRST YEAR CRYPTO BULLION EXCHANGES

Throughout the first year, thirteen known cryptocurrency exchanges initiated live trading of Crypto Bullion. As is evident below, trading of the coin does not occur on any of these now. Almost all the exchanges have closed due to dubious activities, successful hacking attempts or other reasons. Bittrex is the only exchange still operational (it removed Crypto Bullion because the coin had reached a low daily trading volumes there).

The following table lists the dates on which active trading of the coin began:

Cryptocurrency Exchange	Trading Against	Status of Exchange	Date on which Active Trading Began
Coins-e	BTC	CLOSED	1st of July 2013
Cryptsy	BTC and LTC	CLOSED	25th of July 2013
CoinEx	BTC	CLOSED	7th of August 2013
PhenixEx	BTC	CLOSED	4th of August 2013
OpenEx	BTC	CLOSED	9th of January 2014
Cryptokopen	BTC and EUR	CLOSED	1st of February 2014
AllCrypt	BTC	CLOSED	10th of March 2014
Bittrex	BTC	CLOSED	23rd of March 2014
Ecoinfund	BTC and CNY	CLOSED	24th of March 2014
Swaphole	BTC	CLOSED	28th of March 2014
PTOPEX	BTC	CLOSED	5th of April 2014
Vault of Satoshi	BTC, USD and CAD	CLOSED	10th of April 2014
Comkort	BTC	CLOSED	27th of April 2014

CURRENT CRYPTO BULLION EXCHANGES

A cryptocurrency exchange is a site on which registered users can buy or sell Crypto Bullion against BTC, LTC, USD and so on. Some exchanges require users to fully register by submitting certain documentation including proof of identity and address. On the other hand, most exchanges only require users to register with a simple username and password with the use of a currently held e-mail account.

On the 6th of September 2016, there were three known exchanges or methods to buy/sell/trade Crypto Bullion. At this time, Cryptopia was the exchange on which the highest daily trade volume was occurring.

Current cryptocurrency exchanges which actively allow users to trade CBX are:

Exchange	Location	Traded Against
Cryptopia	New Zealand	BTC
YoBit		BTC
Cryptomic		BTC

CRYPTO BULLION TEAM

Crypto Bullion is professionally being developed, marketed and managed by a dedicated team of skilled individuals who want to see the coin succeed. According to the official Crypto Bullion website, there are six individuals who collaborate from countries all around the world. These six individuals are:

Chris "eLambert" - CBX Founder/Developer (USA)

"Founder, developer, capital investor and concept creator. Elambert has been involved with crypto-currencies since 2011 and created the concept for Crypto Bullion to fill a niche as the digital compliment to precious metals. Crypto Bullion is designed to cater to the long-term investor by offering security, stability, ultra-low inflation and interest earnings. Elambert brings with him an extensive background in business management, entrepreneurship and data analysis."

Ben "VonSpass" - Marketing Strategy Director (Canada)

"Instantly recognized the gigantic potential for the Bitcoin protocol upon first hearing about it, he went through the crypto-currency cycle: mining BTC, mining LTC, trading BTC, etc. Ben liked the values of our Crypto Bullion: low inflation, high value and rarity. A University graduate in Marketing, Ben accepted the challenge to bring Crypto Bullion forward. He has a few ideas in store that will bring CBX to the top of all currencies, and hopefully far beyond."

Alexandre "Alex4J" - Senior Coder/Developer (Belgium)

"Alex4J is an initially self taught programmer who later in life pursued professional training and accreditation. Along the way he discovered a passion for cryptography and cryptocurrency and joins the Crypto Bullion Team with a wealth of knowledge and experience in these areas of study and development.

CRYPTO BULLION TEAM

Additional to this, Alex4J brings another flavor of culture to the already diverse development team as well as his associated ideas and familiarity with CBX's target demographic."

Malafaya - Regional Developer (Portugal)

"Cryptocurrency enthusiast and a software programmer. He started with Bitcoin in 2013, and later that year found altcoins and mainly Crypto Bullion. "What impressed me the most about CBX at the time was its sound financial parameters." 2016 marked the start of his active participation in the team as the Regional Developer for Portugal, Brazil and the Portuguese-speaking countries. He also participates occasionally in smaller software development activities for CBX."

Erwin "BTCat" - Director Social Media Marketing (Netherlands)

"Crypto-currency trader, project manager, marketeer and developer on the web. BTCat stumbled upon Bitcoin in early 2013 and Crypto Bullion just after it's launch. "I took notice of CBX because of the friendly and professional approach in communicating with the community. It was the first spark." Since then BTCat has contributed as a volunteer. BTCat is also managing @CryptoTraders on Twitter which he has built to reach over 35k followers…"

Jimmy "JimmyZhu" - Liaison to China (China)

"JimmyZhu is a crypto enthusiast based in China. When a position opened for someone to aid with the entry and adoption of Crypto Billion into the Chinese markets, JimmyZhu was a top responder. Due to his enthusiasm, passion and work ethic, he was selected to fill the Liaison to China position."

CRYPTO BULLION COMMUNITY

A community is a social unit or network that shares common values and goals. It derives from the Old French word "comuntee". This, in turn, originates from "communitas" in Latin (communis; things held in common). Crypto Bullion has a community consisting of an innumerable number of individuals who have the coin's well being and future goal at heart. These individuals almost always prefer fictitious names with optional corresponding "avatars". Notable members of the community are users "elambert", "VonSpass", "BTCat" and others.

At the time of publication, there are social media sites on which discussion and development of Crypto Bullion take place. These are:

- Bitcointalk -https://bitcointalk.org/index.php?topic=951753.0/
- Facebook -https://www.facebook.com/CryptogenicBullion/
- Freenode IRC -http://webchat.freenode.net/?channels=#cryptobullion/
- Official Forum -http://forum.cryptobullion.io/
- Reddit -https://www.reddit.com/r/CryptoBullionX/
- Twitter -https://twitter.com/cryptobullionX/

In essence, the community surrounding and participating in the development of Crypto Bullion is the backbone of the coin. Without a following, the prospects of future adoption and utilisation are starkly limited. Crypto Bullion belongs to all those people who use it, not just to the developers who aid its progression.

FIRST YEAR HISTORY OF CRYPTO BULLION

LIST OF CHAPTERS

JUNE 2013	—LAUNCH OF THE CRYPTO BULLION BLOCKCHAIN
JULY 2013	—FIRST TWO CRYPTOCURRENCY EXCHANGES INITIATED CBX TRADING
AUGUST 2013	—NEW COIN LOGO UNVEILED AND OFFICIAL WEBSITE LAUNCHED
SEPTEMBER 2013	—MARKET CAPITALISATION BEGAN TO SURGE
OCTOBER 2013	—NEW OFFICIAL BLOCK EXPLORER LAUNCHED
NOVEMBER 2013	—FINITEBYDESIGN ONE OUNCE .999 SILVER BARS MADE AVAILABLE
DECEMBER 2013	—ALL TIME HIGH MARKET CAPITALISATION OF CRYPTO BULLION ATTAINED
JANUARY 2014	—NEW PLANS FOR CRYPTO BULLION IN 2014
FEBRUARY 2014	— DIRECTOR OF MARKETING AND STRATEGY USER "PAPERSHEEPDOG" JOINED THE CBX TEAM
MARCH 2014	—LEAD DEVELOPER RESIGNED AND FOUR EXCHANGES INITIATED CBX TRADING
APRIL 2014	—DIRECT FIAT TO CBX TRADING MADE AVAILABLE BY VAULT OF SATOSHI
MAY 2014	—CRYPTOTOWN ON THE GROUND PROJECT
JUNE 2014	—ONE YEAR ANNIVERSARY OF CRYPTO BULLION

JUNE 2013

LAUNCH OF THE CRYPTO BULLION BLOCKCHAIN
JUNE 2013

I. Bitcointalk forum thread created for Crypto Bullion.

II. Block number one timestamped at 17:46:02 UTC on the 27th of June.

III. Pre-mine of 9,339.899 CBX mined.

IV. Blockchain publicly launched at 01:58:08 UTC on the 28th of June.

V. First Crypto Bullion block explorer created thanks to user "diatonic".

On the 28th of June 2013 at 01:22:13 UTC, a Bitcointalk forum thread was created by a user known by the fictitious forum name "elambert". This thread was originally titled "[ANN] Official launch of Cryptogenic Bullion". About eight minutes later, the first response to this thread was posted by user "tadakaluri" who was quoted as saying:

> "Where is the Client.....?"

Another early post was submitted by user "CryptoBullion" at 01:59:33 UTC:

> "Crypto - Genic - Bullion , i like the name"

JUNE 2013

Interestingly, another project related thread (created on the 27th of June at 09:58:38 UTC) had been created before the official Bitcointalk forum thread by user "elambert". It had been created to allow initial followers and passers by to guess the full name of the coin from its original unit of account symbol (CGB). A graphic was posted on the initial post (see page 32). It was correctly guessed by user "The_Catman" and user "elambert" requested that he must download and install the wallet after launch so he would receive his reward.

Originally, the source code was located at the website https://github.com/cryptogenicbonds/CGB.

Block #0 (Reward 0 CBX) June 27th 2013 at 04:52:05 PM UTC

Block #1 (Reward 10 CBX) June 27th 2013 at 05:46:02 PM UTC

As can be seen immediately below, the initial block distribution table had already been established. A total coin circulation cap of one million CBX, a block time of sixty seconds and a difficulty re-targeting time of two minutes were the case.

Initial Block	Final Block	# Blocks	Reward	Total	Cum Total
1	934	934	10	9,340	9,340
935	50,000	49,066	10	490,660	500,000
50,001	100,000	50,000	5	250,000	750,000
100,001	150,000	50,000	2.5	125,000	875,000
150,001	200,000	50,000	1.25	62,500	937,500

It is important to note that a sizeable proportion of these blocks were going to be timestamped by proof of stake, not proof of work. Taking into account that PoS rewards are relatively smaller than PoW rewards, the cumulative totals shown above would, in time, turn out to be lower.

JUNE 2013

> **Block #934 (Reward 10 CBX) June 28th 2013 at 01:53:32 AM UTC**

At block number 934, the pre-mine (coins which went towards the cost of development, bounties and giveaways) had been mined (9,339.899 CBX to be exact) by the development team. All blocks to be mined, beginning at block number 935, could now be mined publicly. As a result, the cryptocurrency community were able to mine the coin and the blockchain had been publicly launched.

On the 28th of June at 03:19:12 UTC, user "diatonic" was quoted as saying:

> "I set up a block explorer at http://cgb.webboise.com:2770
> Please send any bounty or donations to 5dimes5hcuK7WZwNz52No4KurMAb6SqJH7
> Thanks!"

On the 28th of June at 09:19:15 UTC, user "elambert" posted the following:

> "Good morning all! Thank you for your support thru the launch of CGB. It has been a crazy couple of days leading up to this release which I had intended for this morning 5-6am est standard time. However, during the tail end of the pre-mine, someone else was able to tap in and started to mine. In order to prevent an unfair advantage, I was forced to release early in a rush. My apologies to all. The pre-mine plus additional mining after launch yielded a total of 9,399.88 CGB. This will go towards the initial targeted goal of 10,000 CGB pre-mine and will be used for support, development, giveaways and other promotions. This brings the pre-mine (post launch mine included) total to .094% of the total cap. I hope you all have found this launch exciting, fair as possible and I hope all are enjoying mining. I will be giving out CGB's to those that have been helpful to this launch thru-ought this thread. Your efforts are greatly appreciated, will be rewarded and I look to hopefully pull you each in as collaborators going forward - should you be interested. Look for a giveaway thread to start soon as well as the posting of the pre-mine ledger. Get your wallets set up!
>
> Finally, if anyone has constructive criticism, creative ideas or other ways to benefit CGB (or crypto-currencies in general), please pm me or post on one of my threads. I will be happy to use the pre-mine capital to push forward any such beneficial pursuits.
>
> More to come..."

JUNE 2013

In accordance with the conversation on Bitcointalk, user "The_Catman" said:

> "I believe you owe me two rewards for guessing the name of your currency, twice. You may send the rewards to this address: 5X1oqX5oQ8V12Dg9zwoD7mrQGb3FXU5tEY"

On the 28th of June at 10:12:45 UTC, user "elambert" responded:

> "5 CGB sent - Thank you for your support!" 😁

User "elambert" also tipped CBX to the following users who had already posted their wallet addresses on the official Crypto Bullion Bitcointalk thread:

> "The_Catman" - 5 CGB (for guessing the correct name of the coin)
> "techbytes" - 1 CGB (posted their wallet address)
> "Rubberduckie" - 20 CGB
> "marcetin" - 1 CGB (posted their wallet address)
> "The_Catman" - 20 CGB (again for posting the sourcecode link)
> "GoldBit89" - 1 CGB
> "kelsey" - 1 CGB
> "tob101" - 1 CGB
> "tadakaluri" - 1 CGB
> "diatonic" - 20 CGB (set up a block explorer at http://cgb.webboise.com:2770)
> "MobGod" - 50 CGB (set up a lotto site at http://iurl.no/68e47)

There were some people who described the coin as not being innovative. They pointed out its inherent characteristic of being a clone of another previously launched cryptocurrency. Due to its pre-determined scarcity, it was viewed as a vehicle for just making money. Nevertheless, others were keen to participate towards mining the coin and helping the coin progress. There was some initial hatred towards how the founder/developers had set up the announcement and the manner in which information was made available at the beginning.

Consequently, user "elambert" was quoted as saying:

> "Serious hatred in the community, lol.
>
> I do hope you are correct about the success of Phenixcoin as I am heavily invested, however your rush to judgement on CGB worries me about your judgement. Hopefully you are correct 50% of the time, lol
>
> Btw, source posted in ANN now. Sorry for delay, had to rush launch to prevent an information leak from turning destructive."

FIRST TWO CRYPTOCURRENCY EXCHANGES INITIATED CBX TRADING

JULY 2013

I. First cryptocurrency exchange called Coins-e initiated live trading of CBX.

II. Second cryptocurrency exchange called Cryptsy initiated live trading of CBX.

III. Official Crypto Bullion Twitter page created.

IV. An inflation of 1-2 % introduced instead of a static one million total.

V. Official Crypto Bullion Facebook page founded.

About three days after the public launch of the Crypto Billion Blockchain, the first cryptocurrency exchange initiated live trading of the coin against Bitcoin. Known as Coins-e, it was an exchange that had only been operational for approximately two weeks and began with sixteen coins on its trading platform. On the 1st of July at 19:06:57 UTC, user "minus" notified the community of this event on the official Crypto Bullion Bitcointalk thread:

> "Trade Cryptogenic Bullion on Coins-E now!
>
> http://www.coins-e.com/exchange/CGB_BTC/
>
> CGB address:5nSUrCaB3dipbTJPypcvkKY2kNJwsB3NoJ
>
> Cheers"

JULY 2013

On the 3rd of July at 06:07:02 UTC, user "thekidcoin" was quoted as saying:

> "Any word on getting CGB on cryptsy? The coin is mining pretty well, not many stales and haven't seen any orphans. The 1 million coins is IMHO the perfect number for consolidating wealth (if its worth anything in the future). May be a good way to hide from BTC and LTC swings if the price stabilizes (and again, the price goes up of course).
>
> OP any info on pools or other services???"

From the 3rd to the 10th of July, no replies were posted on the official CBX Bitcointalk thread by the founder "elambert". A few users were concerned about his absence and the lack of interest or promotion of the coin. His absence was probably due to his continued commitment to focus on the development of CBX.

On the 10th of July at 20:04:54 UTC, user "elambert" was quoted as saying:

> "Stay tuned. Announcements coming soon. Mine away while difficulty is low, block rewards high and no current listing on major exchange..."

It was therefore the view of the founder that Coins-e was not a major exchange.

On the 12th of July at 14:20:33 UTC, user "elambert" said:

> Please download to correct the "Checkpoint too old warning":
>
> https://docs.google.com/file/d/0B_N4P72HWplSWkw3cnBEel96cVU/edit?usp=sharing
>
> Let me know if anyone has issues with this. Will be making a unique thread to announce this soon with another promotional giveaway shortly...

Despite the availability of the wallet client, the corrected Mac OS X version had not been released. User "maxpower" was a well known and trusted Mac developer who was working to create one. The development team knew it was important to make the wallet client accessible to all people who wanted it, regardless of which operating system they were using.

On the 13th of July at 10:16:22 UTC, user "nullbitspectre1848" asked:

> "So when are we going to start seeing some action with this 'coin'? I have a whack of it now and I want to gamble/spend it. And what's with the seemingly ONE miner that pops in every few hours just to push the difficulty up?"

On the same day at 11:50:03 UTC, user "elambert" replied by saying:

> "Edits have been made to the code to improve the currency and push it to the next level. I will be creating an announcement thread as time allows this weekend, so keep a look out.
>
> I have no answer to your mining question, but I would expect the difficulty to continue to sky rocket so enjoy it while low. It was .05 a few days ago and surged 1400% to .7 yesterday, now floating in the .35 range. All over the map, but as the announcement comes out, I think you will see a rise and stabilization (or continued rise). Stay tuned my friend and thank you for your mining and support!"

On the 14th of July at 19:07:58 UTC, user "miffman" created a thread on Bitcointalk devoted to a CBX giveaway titled "***Free Cryptogenic Bullion*** - giveaway :)". The first fifty people to post their wallet address would then receive 0.1 CBX. Thanks to a donation from Jaaanstorm, the giveaway was extended beyond the initial restriction above. It would not be until the 17th of November 2013 that this thread was locked:

> https://bitcointalk.org/index.php?topic=256234

JULY 2013

On the 18th of July at 01:54:26 UTC, user "elambert" made the following announcement:

> IRC issue fixed! Please download the new binaries below:
>
> Windows QT/Daemon:
> https://docs.google.com/file/d/0B_N4P72HWpISakFtTVJNU1IScms/edit?usp=sharing
>
> Linux 32 QT/Daemon:
> https://docs.google.com/file/d/0B_N4P72HWpISN0RzdG0xQ195VlE/edit?usp=sharing
>
> Linux 64 QT/Daemon:
> https://docs.google.com/file/d/0B_N4P72HWpISMlJuRXkxc0VnZ2c/edit?usp=sharing
>
> OP updated!
> ~ Team CGB

Thanks were given to user "thekidcoin" who had helped to solve these problems. The IRC server originally used was banning everyone and people thought "bots" were to blame.

Six days later, the Mac wallet client update was released. Also on this day (late UTC), the founder "elambert" made the following offer:

> "OP updated with solo mining info. Still bounties available for someone who has time and wants to make a step by step guide for solo mining CGB. This manual should be easy enough for someone new to computers to be able to follow and get mining. My wife will test it out, lol. 50 CGB for Mac and 50 CGB for Windows, or 100 CGB if you do both."

Less than one hour later on the 25th of July, user "mercSuey" directly responded to the post immediately above. He had posted a short guide to solo mining which contained the necessary information for anyone interested. He did not, however, want the bounty offered. This guide was later added to the opening post of the original (historical) Crypto Bullion Bitcointalk forum thread.

On the 25th of July at 23:14:43 UTC, user "BitJohn" was quoted as saying:

> "Welcome CGB fans to the cryptsy.com family"

It was the second cryptocurrency exchange to add Crypto Bullion. Founded on the 20th of May 2013, Cryptsy was based in Delray Beach, Florida, USA. Direct trades of CBX against Bitcoin were the seventieth market to be added to Cryptsy:

Cryptsy
http://www.cryptsy.com/markets/view/70

In the early hours (UTC) of the 26th of July, user "elambert" said:

> "Thank you BitJohn! It is like coming home to family after a long time away!"

After 970 days in operation, the exchange closed its doors to live trading on the 14th of January 2016. On this day, the last recorded trades of CBX resulted in a low of 31,000, an open of 37,960, a close of 31,000 and a high of 37,960 Bitcoin Satoshi (daily trading volume 149.85 CBX). There were reports they had gone bankrupt due to an earlier heist of a large amount of Bitcoin and Litecoin (millions of US$). Unfortunately, many people were unable to withdraw their deposits.

On the 28th of July at 13:41:52 UTC, user "elambert" said:

> "Subsidy should be halving in a couple of days and the website launch is scheduled to coincide with this event. Additional services will be coming to light in the month of August, stay tuned!"

JULY 2013

A question was submitted concerning the next move of the coin. On the 28th of July at 13:49:08 UTC, user "mercSuey" gave his own personal opinion:

> "First step is securing the blockchain, especially until PoS blocks kick in. If the primary goal for CGB is to be a investment vehicle for multiplying the value appreciation of BTC, blockchain security is of utmost importance.
>
> I'm developing a Android wallet as well as a gaming site that will accept only BTC, LTC, CGB, and CAP. And we're going to heavily market CGB as a high-roller cryptocurrency. Exclusivity because of its rarity, yet practical because of its block time for quick transaction confirmations and liquidity due to its one million coin cap.
>
> -Merc"

Also on this day, proof of stake blocks were successfully being timestamped to the blockchain for the first time. Taking into account that proof of stake blocks, more often than not, have a lower reward (stake), this would result in less than 500,000 CBX generated at block number 50,000.

On the following day, an official Twitter Account was created for the coin at https://twitter.com/CryptogenicBull. This account is no longer accessible.

On the 30th of July at 11:53:00 UTC, user "elambert" said:

> "OP updated:
> July 30th, 2013 Update:
>
> Please download the updated clients (in OP). Also a couple of changes have been made to take preventative measures against what recently occurred with CAP. Finally, the block rewards have been extended to allow for a 1/2% yearly inflation after 1 million CGB are mined - at a rate of 0.01 CGB per block:
> DNS seeds have been enable and DNS records have been created which resolve to 6 trusted nodes (we will add more soon)
> Checkpoints added
> Added reward of 0.01 CGB after 1 million coins are mined (comes out to 1/2% yearly inflation)"

On the 31st of July, user "mercSuey" was taking the lead on the project. It was left to him to share news/updates about the new upcoming official CBX website. Also on the last day of the month at 17:26:57 UTC, user "sharkbyte093" said:

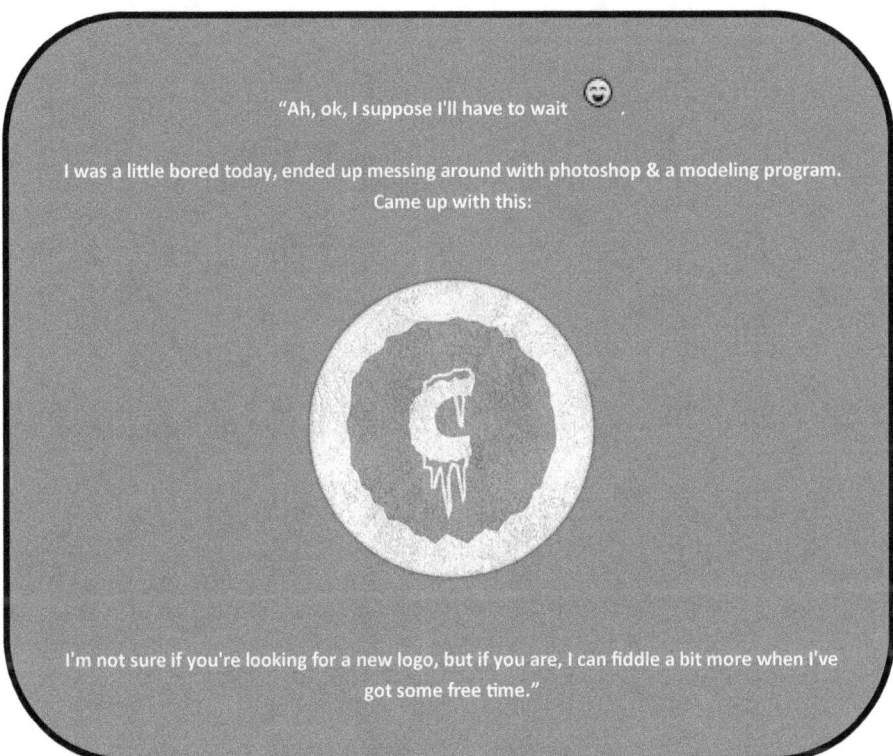

There was anticipation of the PoW block reward halving from 10 CBX to 5 CBX at block number 50,001. However, at block number 50,001, no halving occurred.

The total number of generated coins surpassed 500,000 CBX at block number 50,064 on the 31st July at 21:47:41 UTC.

Block #50,000 (Reward 10 CBX) July 31st 2013 at 08:39:14 PM UTC

Block #50,001 (Reward 10 CBX) July 31st 2013 at 08:41:03 PM UTC

虚拟商品Cryptogenic Bullion，使您的比特币价值成倍增长。

NEW COIN LOGO UNVEILED AND OFFICIAL WEBSITE LAUNCHED

AUGUST 2013

I. PoW block reward halved from 10 CBX to 5 CBX at block number 55,001.

II. Crypto Bullion added to the website at www.coinmarketcap.com.

III. Third cryptocurrency exchange called CoinEx initiated active trading of CBX.

IV. A new coin logo design unveiled.

V. Official website went live at http://cryptogenicbullion.org.

As soon as it was noticed that no block halving (from ten to five CBX) had occurred at block number 50,001, the developers checked, updated and released a new wallet client. On the 1st of August at 09:55:34 UTC, user "elambert" posted the following announcement:

> "August 1, 2013 Update: *Yesterday was truly an interesting day for CGB and the crypto community! The subsidy halving set to take place at 50k blocks did not occur due to an oversight in the code. The CGB team has responded, identified the issue and made the necessary corrections. The subsidy halving will now take place at block 55k. It is imperative that everyone download the latest client BEFORE block 55k. We apologize for the inconvenience and appreciate your continued support. Please be prepared for some additional major announcements coming for CGB!*
>
> Please download the updated client on OP."

AUGUST 2013

In a similar fashion to before, user "maxpower" compiled the Mac OS X wallet client. It was added to the opening post of the official CBX Bitcointalk thread later on the 1st of August. Also on this day at 11:01:30 UTC, user "Lauda", in reference to the recent wallet client update, said:

> "Good job fixing it quickly!"

On the 2nd of August at 09:10:03 UTC, user "elambert" was quoted as saying:

> "I hope everyone has updated their client before the 55k fork. If not, please do so immediately! I am in the EST and figure that as we cross over into Sunday, the fork should occur. Don't want anyone to lose the correct block chain. BTW, it is FRIDAY!!!"

On the same day at 14:43:56 UTC, a separate Bitcointalk thread titled "500 CGB BOUNTY!!! New CGB Logo Design Contest!" was created. All members were free to submit designs there until the closing date on the 10th of August.

On the 4th of August, the block reward of each PoW block changed from 10 CBX to 5 CBX. There were people who expected a quick rise in the Bitcoin Satoshi price of one unit of CBX account.

> Block #55,000 (Reward 10 CBX) August 4th 2013 at 08:13:35 AM UTC

> Block #55,001 (Reward 5 CBX) August 4th 2013 at 08:13:58 AM UTC

Also on the 4th of August, Crypto Bullion was added to a website which ranks cryptocurrencies in descending order of market capitalisation. In this sense, the market capitalisation is the total value of all coins ever generated for that particular cryptocurrency. On the website at www.coinmarketcap.com, the initial value of the market capitalisation and the Bitcoin Satoshi value of one unit of CBX account were $51,669 and 89,802 respectively.

On the 5th of August at 17:49:58 UTC, user "elambert" made an announcement:

> "August 5, 2013 Update:
>
> The CGB team is pleased to announce an improved client! We have identified and fixed an issue with the PoS reward system as well as added in new security checkpoints. In order to give users an opportunity to update their clients, we have set this update to take place at block number 59,700. This block will occur Wednesday morning in EST time. Please update your clients immediately! We apologize for the inconvenience and had contemplated holding back on this update, however, we determined that the benefits outweighed the hassle and this was best handled right away.
>
> Please download the updated clients in OP."

Besides individual wallet client users downloading and installing the new version, exchanges, mining pools and block explorers had to too. Both Coins-e and Cryptsy updated before block number 59,700. User "diatonic" was notified so he was able to make sure the block explorer he created would be on the correct chain.

Also on the 5th of August, the coin logo design contest was heating up.

Two days later, block number 59,700 was timestamped. From this point in time, the recently identified problems with proof of stake were resolved:

Block #59,700 (Reward 5 CBX) August 7th 2013 at 05:34:48 PM UTC

On the 7th of August, live trading of CBX began on the cryptocurrency exchange called CoinEx. This was the third exchange to add CBX, but no longer exists. On the 17th of March 2014, they were hacked. Soon after this event, they closed their doors. Fortunately, some users were able to withdraw funds from there.

On the same day at 21:21:50 UTC, user "elambert" said:

> "Great news! A new exchange! OP updated."

AUGUST 2013

On the 10th of August, the coin logo design contest ended. During the preceding eight day period, the following were some of the submitted designs:

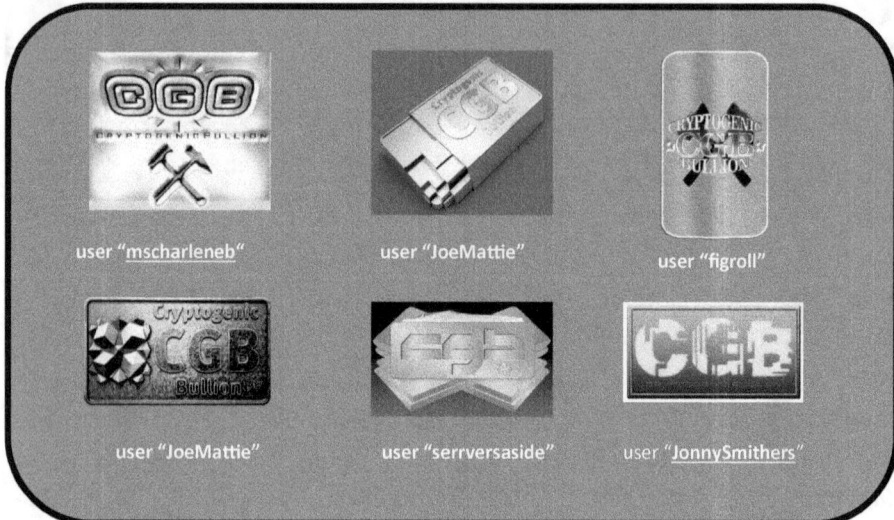

A decision was made by the development team to blend the designs of user "JoeMattie" (bullion bar) and user "Cryptasm" (brand logo). This design can be seen below on the left. User "elambert" admitted it was not an easy contest as it could have gone in numerous directions. It was initially intended for there to be one winner. Instead, a total prize fund of 1,495 CBX was rewarded and shared between about one dozen people. Users "JoeMattie" and "Cryptasm" each received 500 CBX. Thanks were given to all those artists who had participated.

As well as the winning coin logo design, an official website for Crypto Bullion went live. To celebrate this event, user "elambert" created a separate Bitcointalk thread titled "Cryptogenic Bullion Website Launched!!! August 10, 2013". On the 10th of August at 23:53:26 UTC, he was quoted as saying:

> "The Cryptogenic Bullion Team is thrilled to announce the launch of our highly anticipated website!
>
> Special thanks and credit to Mercsuey who has worked tirelessly to build this site for the Cryptogenic Bullion community!
>
> http://CryptogenicBullion.org"

A quote from the official website was:

> "Cryptogenic Bullion—With an emphasis on security and marketing; we aim to provide a true virtual commodity to satisfy strategic business needs."

On the 16th of August at 00:03:12 UTC, user "elambert" was quoted as saying:

> "OP updated.
>
> New Binaries - 8.15.13
> New checkpoints and new logos!"

This updated version of the wallet client (v 1.1.5.3) was optional. It was released merely for aesthetic purposes as it included the winning coin logo design and splash screen image. Later on the same day, the Mac OS X version was released.

On the following day, permission was given to anyone who wished to use the images shown on page 46. Avatars and screensavers were some suggestions of how they could be used.

AUGUST 2013

On the 19th of August at 16:17:27 UTC, user "mercSuey" created a separate Bitcointalk thread in order to advertise new "Cryptogenic Bullion Accepted Here" images. He encouraged people to use these on their sites if they were accepting CBX as a means of payment. The opening post was:

"New 'Cryptogenic Bullion Accepted Here' images!

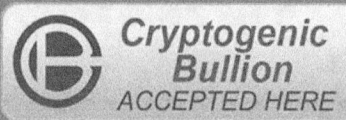

Also, would like to announce a few recent services accepting CB as payment:

Auction website accepting CB: http://cgb.bit4coin.com/

Multi-coin payment processor: https://coinpayments.net/

Marketing and PR services firm (we're also a client): http://bitcoinPRbuzz.com

Things are moving along quite nicely! More to come, so stay tuned!

http://CryptogenicBullion.org"

On the 22nd of August at 08:55:52 UTC, user "FiniteByDesign" said:

> "My web store specializing in .999 Fine Silver - Jewelry and Govt Issue Mint Coins accepts CB as a payment option.
>
> Check us out at:
> http://www.finitebydesign.com
>
> New merchandise continues to be added and a big surprise for the community will be announced before the weekend!
>
> https://bitcointalk.org/index.php?topic=278470.0"

Crypto Bullion was beginning to attract the attention of online merchandisers such as FiniteByDesign. This news was welcomed by the community as a whole.

Other events which occurred in the month of August were:

- On the 13th of August, a Dutch translation of the official CBX website went live.

- On the 16th of August, a Facebook Advertisement Campaign was launched. If seen, user "elambert" encouraged members of the community to post a screenshot of it.

- A Chinese version of the official website was launched on the 18th of August at http://CryptogenicBullion.org/index_chinese.html. As a result of the Chinese website launch, the founder updated the opening post to include the hyperlink. He also did this with every other useful website or mining pool. (中文版网站正式发布！).

- On the 25th of August, a Google Adwords Campaign began in order to promote the coin.

- On the 30th of August, the official CBX Facebook Page surpassed 4,000 likes for the first time.

Crypto Bullion—History of the First Year

MARKET CAPITALISATION BEGAN TO SURGE
SEPTEMBER 2013

I. PoW block reward halved from 5 CBX to 2.5 CBX at block number 95,001.

II. Market capitalisation surpassed $250,000 for the first time.

III. Market capitalisation began to surge.

IV. Yahoo Finance article published.

V. Version 1.1.6.3 of the wallet client released.

At the very beginning of the month, user "mercSuey" officially announced that an advanced and aggressive marketing campaign began during the previous month. The cost of advertising on sites such as Facebook, Yahoo/Bing and Google Adwords had already exceeded $1,000 from his own pocket. He envisaged this to increase throughout September. His objective was to further promote Crypto Bullion, therefore expand the community.

On the 1st of September, the reward of each PoW block halved for a second time:

Block #95,000 (Reward 5 CBX) September 1st 2013 at 10:12:42 AM UTC

Block #95,001 (Reward 2.5 CBX) September 1st 2013 at 10:12:50 AM UTC

SEPTEMBER 2013

As soon as block number 95,000 was timestamped to the blockchain, there were a total of 725,496.77366419 CBX which had been mined.

Also on the 1st of September at 10:18:52 UTC, user "elambert" said:

> "Subsidy just halved! Looks good. Mining profitability halved as well so this leaves room for price increase before activation of the large pools that move between currencies finding the most profitable one to mine and dump."

Topics discussed at the beginning of the month concerned an official Crypto Bullion forum and a vanity wallet generator website. User "mercSuey" was working on creating a forum which was planned to go live within the next week or so. However, this never became reality.

On the website www.coinmarketcap.com, Crypto Bullion had reached a market capitalisation (the total fiat value of all CBX in existence) of about $200,000. In doing so, it was ranked at 12th position on the 3rd of September. On this day at 18:03:01 UTC, user "LaudaM" posted the following:

> "Due to the low number of coins it's easy to get the price up. We are on the way into the top 10 " 😃 😄

Just under forty minutes later, user "miffman" notified the community that this had become true:

> "we are in the top 10! amazing!!
>
> 10   Cryptogenic Bullion $ 250,557 $ 0.34   733,589 CGB   +69.74 %"

On the 4th of September at 10:01:07 UTC, user "elambert" said:

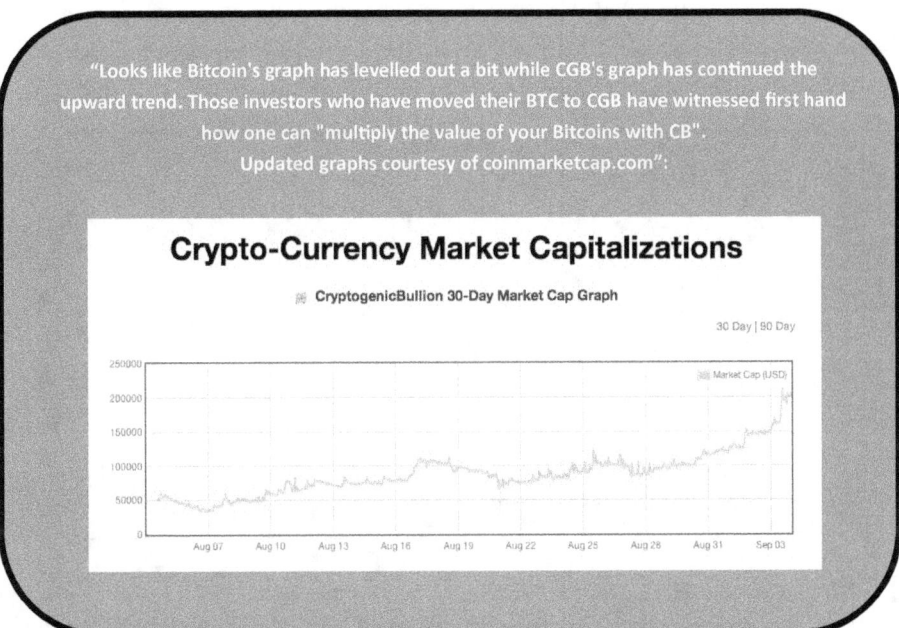

"Looks like Bitcoin's graph has levelled out a bit while CGB's graph has continued the upward trend. Those investors who have moved their BTC to CGB have witnessed first hand how one can "multiply the value of your Bitcoins with CB".
Updated graphs courtesy of coinmarketcap.com":

During the past several days, the Bitcoin Satoshi value of one unit of Crypto Bullion account had been surging to new highs on Cryptsy:

	Price	Low	Open	Close	High	Volume (BTC)
31st Aug	121,900.5	121,610	121,701	122,100	130,000	16.4847
1st Sept	133,600.5	122,001	122,100	145,101	157,999	31.3006
2nd Sept	150,024.5	145,005	149,494	150,100	157,600	19.9295
3rd Sept	175,602	150,100	150,100	201,104	262,010	82.3298
4th Sept	207,553.5	180,000	201,104	214,003	261,000	87.2895
11th Sept	312,607	300,001	310,214	315,000	337,000	18.1227

source: www.cryptocoincharts.info

SEPTEMBER 2013

On the 5th of September, user "kriwest" thought the official CBX website lacked professionalism in terms of the graphics used and how they were presented. He was concerned that user "mercSuey" was not making the website an important marketing tool for CBX. A response was posted by user "mercSuey" who said:

> "Our attention is on more pressing development matters of the blockchain at the moment. At this point, with the rise in market cap value, we have an intense pressure to deliver on project announcements. I suspect that producing actual innovation to the blockchain will be more marketable and inspire much more confidence than a pretty website. But in time, the website will get a complete face-lift, so to keep things fresh.
>
> On another note, CB's Facebook page hit 5400 likes. And we've seen a nice spike in likes the past couple days, which I assume is related to the price spike in CB. Our marketing slogan, "Multiply the value of your bitcoins with CB", which can be seen at the top of CCN http://www.cryptocoinsnews.com/ is proving to be truth as both CB and BTC have simultaneously risen in value. We're obviously doing something right.
>
> I want to support our supporters and the only way I know how to do that is to code and develop and try to push the envelope and set the standard in open source altcoin innovation.
>
> -Merc"

User "mercSuey" emphasised how important the next couple of months would be to the continued success of the coin. He was very appreciative of the great support from the community and emphasised his own commitment not to let the Crypto Bullion Community down.

On the 7th of September at 09:24:54 UTC, user "elambert" said:

> "It looks like some serious investors are getting involved in CB. It is not easy to pick up a large volume without pushing up the price. I have noticed that the price gets pushed up as investors load up and then the buying slows for a bit for new sell orders to leak into the spread between buy and sell - then the process repeats. I have also noticed that the buyers are not screaming "pump" in the chat box, they are trying to buy without being noticed."

On the 7th of September at 16:22:09 UTC, user "mercSuey" said:

> "Guys, Please forgive me for not working on vanity address and forum. I want to concentrate all my resources on our major projects we have scheduled for release in the next two months. I'd like to get them released and then work on the forum/vanity address generator afterwards, to support the resulting interest from the new project releases. The quicker I can get these projects released then the quicker we justify the price rise, which is important to me.
>
> -Merc"

There were members of the community who understood the priorities which user "mercSuey" had chosen. If there were more important tasks to be dealt with, he was encouraged to focus on those first. Besides development of the paper wallet generator falling through, this was also the case with an official forum. Someone else was sought after to create an official forum which would then serve as a much better organiser for discussions than the CBX Bitcointalk thread.

On the 10th of September, a news article was published on Yahoo Finance titled "The Rare, Interest Bearing, Bitcoin Alternative – Cryptogenic Bullion". It can be found in the appendix. What follows is the first paragraph of the article:

> "The number of professional online services incorporating Cryptogenic Bullion is growing at a rapid rate and the currency is currently trading for approximately 500 CGB per 1 BTC. A fork of the virtual currency Novacoin, Cryptogenic Bullion is designed to be a rare, interest bearing, peer-to-peer virtual commodity with the same decentralised characteristics of Bitcoin but with some key differences. Cryptogenic Bullion's innovations include an accelerated decrease of the mining subsidy, almost immediate transaction time and 2% annual interest eligible for Bullion that has been stationary in a user's wallet for at least 30 days. Cryptogenic Bullion has been well received in the digital currency ecosystem. The official Facebook page has over 4,500 fans, and the official CGB website has been translated into Dutch and Chinese."

On the following day, the Bitcoin Satoshi value of one unit of CBX account peaked at a high of 337,000 on Cryptsy (see bottom of table on page 57 for this new high). This high would not be surpassed until the 10th of October 2013.

SEPTEMBER 2013

On the 15th of September at 23:04:05 UTC, user "mercSuey" posted the following:

> "Hello everyone,
>
> Apologies for not being on here more frequently. We're just exceptionally busy with project development, among other things. We have rearranged our marketing budget and put more emphasis on Google Adwords, and consequently decreased the Facebook budget. We have noticed a much stronger correlation between Google Adword clicks and CB price action on Cryptsy, so we wanted to reinforce that correlation. The marketing budget is still on pace to exceed $2000 per month.
>
> In case you missed it, we had some PR crossing the wires last week. Here's the Yahoo News link. Very exciting for the CB community! http://finance.yahoo.com/news/rare-interest-bearing-bitcoin-alternative-091800738.html
>
> We have captured the top ad spot for http://www.cryptonerd.co and we wish good luck to pr9me with his new cryptocoin news service.
>
> We have renewed the top ad spot for http://cryptocoinsnews.com and they have recently remodeled much of their site. Check it out if you haven't already!
>
> These services are so important for the industry as they are, and will be, the main sources of information for everyone and anyone interested in crypto currencies/commodities. I hope many more sprout up, each with their own niche. I definitely feel the market economics of this media space could support many players.
>
> We have received Swedish and Turkish translations of http://CryptogenicBullion.org and we'll implementing them this week.
>
> That's all for now. Please don't hesitate to pm me or elambert if you have any questions or concerns or ideas.
>
> -Merc"

On the following day, user "elambert" created a separate Bitcointalk thread titled "Use CGB's advertising budget to market your goods and services / CGB awards???" on which he was willing to support people who were considering to use CBX as a means of payment to buy/sell their own goods/services. He wanted people to private message him so that collaboration could take place.

During the next few days, several users were reporting issues with the wallet client. User "mercSuey" was working on a new client ready for release soon. On the 27th of September at 08:05:34 UC, user "mercSuey" posted:

> "Greetings! Updated client. changes:
> -updated checkpoints, modified/updated seed and changed splash page to keep things fresh.
>
> ...(DOWNLOAD LINKS)...
>
> I'll have Linux builds released soon, but the github is updated. Mac client will be released within 24 hours.
> Cheers! -Merc"

As promised, both updates for Linux and Mac were released within the next twenty four hours. All corresponding download links were added to the opening post of the official Crypto Bullion Bitcointalk thread by user "elambert".

On the 30th of September at 02:34:49 UTC, user "mercSuey" said:

> "There's nothing to fix per say, we're analyzing the situation as PoW subsidy halves and PoS block frequency increases and takes over the blockchain, as planned. Once the PoW subsidy reaches the baseline .01, it will be extremely inefficient, since PoS blocks overrule PoW blocks. But the plan from the start was to have CB PoW fully mined and running only on PoS. We have several plans ready to be implemented to assure a lower bound in the PoS block frequency so that we can guarantee the transactions will move. Other than that, these are just growing pains as we analyze the behavior, use testnet on the side to continue to experiment with development ideas, and eventually we'll have the tweaks so that the blockchain is in the sweet spot.
>
> -Merc"

Other events which occurred in the month of September were:

- On the 5th of September, CBX began active trading on the exchange called Phenixex. However, it shutdown 24 days later due to technical faults.
- Turkish version of the official website went live on the 24th of September.

NEW OFFICIAL BLOCK EXPLORER LAUNCHED
OCTOBER 2013

I. PoW block reward halved from 2.5 CBX to 1.25 CBX.

II. Blog added to the official Crypto Bullion website.

III. Value of one unit of CBX account reached $0.50.

IV. Official CBX Block Explorer launched at explorer.cryptogenicbullion.org.

V. Official website re-designed and content changed.

As initially planned, the development team were researching the possibility of becoming the first PoS only crypto commodity and phasing out PoW. Would PoS alone be sufficient to confirm transactions in an acceptable timeframe? From block number 129,889 to 137,962 (~16 days), the following occurred:

- 977 PoS blocks occurred during this time frame
- Average time between PoS blocks was 8 minutes ranging from less than 1 minute to 2h 36m
- Only 3 of the 977 blocks were spaced by > 1hr (69 min, 70 min and 156 min respectively)
    - 25% occurred within 2 minutes of the previous PoS block
    - 52% occurred within 5 minutes of the previous PoS block
    - 72% occurred within 10 minutes of the previous PoS block
    - 83% occurred within 15 minutes of the previous PoS block
    - 89% occurred within 20 minutes of the previous PoS block
    - 96% occurred within 30 minutes of the previous PoS block

OCTOBER 2013

The development team viewed proof of working mining as the means to quickly produce the vast majority of coins and proof of stake to sustain the 1-2% inflation.

On the 2nd of October at 14:46:10 UTC, user "hypersire" said:

> "Wow, this is big news indeed! I fully support CB going POS only. Once that happens, I think a good course of action would be to kick the advertising campaign into the next gear and focus on the improvements that CB has over Bitcoin. For example, "CryptogenicBullion - Like Bitcoin, only with interest and no mining!"
>
> The interest-bearing, environmentally-friendly aspects of the POS-only scheme must be at the forefront of the advertising as this is what makes CB truly unique in the sea of alt-coins.
>
> Keep up the great work Team CB!"

Fours days later, the reward of each proof of work block halved for the third time:

Block #145,000 (Reward 2.5 CBX) October 6th 2013 at 11:17:18 AM UTC

Block #145,001 (Reward 1.25 CBX) October 6th 2013 at 11:17:59 AM UTC

On the 7th of October at 12:34:58 UTC, user "elambert" said:

> "Looks like BCT is back after taking a brief vacation.
> Couple quick updates for the CB commuinity:
> CGB subsidy halved again about 24 hours ago so the current
> PoW reward is 1.25 CGB per block
>
> Blog section added to CB website: http://cryptogenicbullion.org/blog.html"

Also on the 7th of October, user "mercSuey" was working to create a new exclusive block explorer for CBX. To complement the sporadically unreliable one created by user "diatonic" earlier in the year, he promised it would go live in the next few days. He chose the hosting domain explorer.cryptogenicbullion.org.

OCTOBER 2013

On the 10th of October, the value of one unit of CBX account surpassed the high reached during the previous month:

	Price	Low	Open	Close	High	Volume (BTC)
10th Oct	294,051	267,880	268,100	320,002	409,999	64.3857

source: www.cryptocoincharts.info

On the 13th of October at 13:41:46 UTC, user "mercSuey" said:

> "Hi,
>
> Although I've got more housekeeping to do with one of our new nodes, I wanted to bring the block explorer back now rather than later. I'll set up a FastCGI explorer later and make it the primary explorer and this explorer will eventually be a backup:
>
> http://explorer.cryptogenicbullion.org:2750/chain/CryptogenicBullion
>
> Cheers! -Merc"

One hour later, user "elambert" praised user "mercSuey" for his ability to squeeze the above into his busy schedule.

On the 17th of October at 17:45:45 UTC, user "elambert" was quoted as saying:

> "Couple quick announcements for the community:
>
> - CB is no longer advertising on the main banner of CryptoCoinNews. We have decided not to renew and instead to redirect the funds that were being used for advertising on CCN to the Google Ad budget as this strategy is proving to get CB exposed to a far larger cross-section of people and businesses.
>
> - Don't forget about the annual contest to reward CB innovation from the community: https://bitcointalk.org/index.php?topic=295534.msg3171405#msg3171405
>
> - Behind the scenes work continues and we will be making a big announcement soon..."

OCTOBER 2013

On the 19th of October at 11:25:57 UTC, user "Sustainable" said:

> "I'm a huge supporter of this currency can't wait for the announcements
>
> $ 436,231
> $ 0.51   860,230 CGB"

Since the launch of the coin roughly fifteen weeks ago, it had established itself as a top ten market capitalisation cryptocurrency without being present on exchanges regarded as being major at the time. These included exchanges such as mcxNOW, Mt Gox and BTC-e. User "elambert" was pleased to have user "mercSuey" on board as the lead developer of CBX, and continued to praise his hard work, enthusiasm and dedication.

Plans were afoot to improve upon many aspects of Crypto Bullion.

On the 19th of October at 13:16:36 UTC, user "mercSuey" said:

> "The rate of CGB/BTC was about .0025-.0026 when BTC/USD was around $150 - $160. And when BTC/USD hit $195 (about a 20% increase), CGB/BTC hit .0021 (about a 20% decrease). So the net value is nearly unchanged, as Killiz said.
>
> The correlation with BTC is accurate and I suspect it will stabilize and be less pressured with each subsidy halving going forward, which was the point of the design of accelerated subsidy halving. I have said all along to those who know me (and a couple times in these forums) that I expect BTC/USD to be over $1000 within a year. And as BTC/USD tests the $200 level, suddenly accelerated subsidy halving looks like a bright idea. Plus, couple that with future project developments of mine as well as a developing economic web ecosystem and continued marketing initiative, then you truly have the potential to--wait for it--multiply the value of your bitcoins over time.
>
> Try not to get caught up with the daily price movements....it will drive you mad.
>
> In the meantime, I believe BTC/USD over $200 will soon have a rising tide raises (most) boats effect and I'm doing my best to make sure CGB is one of those boats.
>
> -Merc"

On the 21st of October at 20:40:36 UTC, user "elambert" said:

> "Day traders dump and when BTC corrects, you better believe they will dump just the same. I have said from the start that CGB is designed for long term holding. It is a quality product - speed, interest bearing, hybrid design for 51% resistance and energy efficiency, rarity, top notch difficulty adjustment algorithm, phenomenal community, solid dev team, services and initiatives, etc. CGB will be fine. No one said this would always be an easy journey, but we will be successful, that is for sure. Still a top 10 market cap currency at this point so little has changed other than BTC flexing - and as we all know, BTC is the key to the door of mass adoption. Let BTC do its thing and open the door, then CGB will slide in behind it. Personally I am invested in CGB to get out of the day-trading game and thus far the results are phenomenal. Try not to get caught up in the swings. I have done that in the past and it never turns out good. Hang in there and I think you will be very pleased with the result
>
> Edit:
>
> Lets assume a truly parabolic explosion occurs with BTC - even to $1000! That is about 500% growth from current standing and involves another $10 billion of new money. In order to match the same growth, CGB only has to have $1.5 million of new money injected and jump from a price of .35 cents to $1.75. Not sure which you think is more likely to be met and exceeded, but I feel confident in my analysis."

Besides other important projects, user "mercSuey" was in the process of upgrading the official website. In particular, he was going to change the text content present there. Another major priority at the time was to establish a market for CBX in China. Interest in Bitcoin had grown substantially there and showed no sign of abating. By working hard and exercising patience, the developers were confident of "making waves in the industry" to push CBX forward.

On the 23rd of October at 12:54:04 UTC, user "elambert" said:

> "Current PoW subsidy will continue to halve after every 50k blocks until it reaches a baseline of 0.01 CGB per block, where it will remain in perpetuity. We are researching and testing the possibilities of discontinuing PoW and running solely on PoS, but no decision has been made on this at this time."

OCTOBER 2013

On the 28th of October at 22:53:13 UTC, user "Killiz" said:

> "Thanks Merc you are doing a great job.
>
> It's easy to forget the CB dev team are just investors in CB like the rest of us, all the time they spend on this project is personal time spent for free, no salary or wage, just done for the benefit of us all. So much has been done already in such a short space of time by only a team of 3. Things happen when they are meant to happen, and at the right time.
>
> CB is a long term investment with the potential of high rewards for all who invest now. CB has a long road ahead, and it will take long term development to reach its destination. Rushing ahead into unknown territory without knowing what is around each corner will only set you back at each obstacle you encounter. The CB Team is wise to this and like to plan ahead.
>
> I am one for waiting, as I know what comes to those who wait"

In response to a concern about the future rarity and inflation of the CBX supply, user "elambert" at 13:07:14 UTC posted a comment. The user who had the concern said the coin specification had changed since the launch:

> "No change, has always been PoS/PoW hybrid - which means coin generation/inflation will continue based on the PoS plus the PoW baseline of .01 will remain. This is why it is and has always been clearly identified on the website as follows (please note the projected supply at the end of 2013 and 2014):
>
> **VIRTUAL COMMODITY VS. VIRTUAL CURRENCY:**
> The key feature that differentiates CB from Bitcoin and other virtual currencies is its rapid decrease of newly minted CB. A comparison of the coin supply growth of CB with other virtual currencies will put into context its proposed rarity:
>
> | currency | projected supply by end of 2013 | projected supply by end of 2014 |
> |---|---|---|
> | Bitcoin | 11,937,575 | 13,251,575 |
> | Litecoin | 23,618,750 | 34,130,750 |
> | Feathercoin | 28,930,800 | 70,978,800 |
> | Peercoin | 21,128,479 | 23,474,907 |
> | CB | 1,000,000 | 1,025,000 |
>
> Please let me know if you have any questions on this. Thanks!"

Other events which occurred in the month of October were:

- On the 2nd of October, the total number of likes of the official CBX Facebook Page surpassed 9,000 likes.

- On the 6th of October, a blog section was added to the official website for a better communication of development plans. One of the first topics of discussion was "One of our main concentrations lately has been analysing Proof-of-Stake (PoS) sustainability versus the one minute block time of our Proof-of-Work (PoW) scheme…".

- On the 10th of October, an online merchandiser called FiniteByDesign made white CBX T-shirts available for sale (see page 62).

- On the 24th of October, the official website of Crypto Bullion at http://cryptogenicbullion.org/index.html was successfully redesigned by user "mercSuey". He was praised by the community.

- On the 29th of October, user "yogg" introduced a CBX specific "altdice game" at http://cgb.aldice.net similar to the early version of Satoshi Dice.

- On the 30th of October, the official CBX Subreddit was created at www.reddit.com/r/CryptogenicBullion/.

FINITEBYDESIGN ONE OUNCE .999 SILVER BARS MADE AVAILABLE NOVEMBER 2013

I. Three Crypto Bullion related products for sale at FiniteByDesign.

II. Version 1.1.6.4 of the wallet client released.

III. PoW block reward halved from 1.25 CBX to 0.625 CBX.

IV. Market capitalisation surpassed $1,000,000 for the first time.

V. A wiki site devoted to all things Crypto Bullion was suggested.

An online merchandiser called FiniteByDesign had helped to promote Crypto Bullion over the last month or so. According to their website, they focus on providing unique, crypto-currency related gifts and collectibles using the finest quality materials. At present, three related CBX products for sale there are:

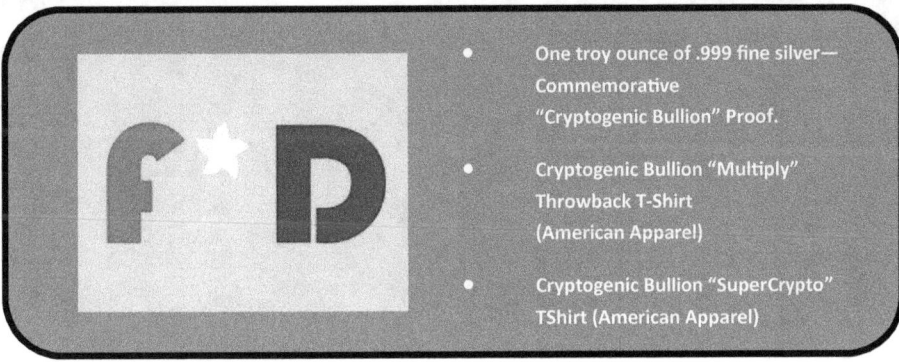

- One troy ounce of .999 fine silver—Commemorative "Cryptogenic Bullion" Proof.
- Cryptogenic Bullion "Multiply" Throwback T-Shirt (American Apparel)
- Cryptogenic Bullion "SuperCrypto" TShirt (American Apparel)

NOVEMBER 2013

On the 5th of November at 14:37:42 UTC, user "mercSuey" said:

> "Hello all,
>
> Updated client (v1.1.6.4) with updated checkpoint, as well as transaction message truncation integrated from bitcoin code that the bitcoin devs implemented a couple months ago as a anti-ddos/less-block-bloat fix. Let me know if any issues arise. Mac build within 48 hours.
>
> Since there's an updated checkpoint, I suggest deleting everything in your data folder EXCEPT your wallet.dat and CryptogenicBullion.conf files. REPEAT: Do not touch the wallet.dat file, or else you'll lose your coins (unless you have a backup!). So, if you don't have a backup of your wallet.dat file, then please do it now. Make a copy and put it in a flash drive for safe keeping. When you run the new client, you'll see the blockchain downloading from the beginning and your balance will be unconfirmed/wrong. Don't be alarmed, the value will be correct and confirmed once the complete blockchain has been downloaded.
>
> Download links below. I started a new github but the old github has been updated. Please use the new github as the old one will be phased out.
> ...(DOWNLOAD LINKS)...
>
> Quick marketing update. I've temporarily scaled back the marketing budget as I continue to develop and prepare for major projects; this includes trying to increase CB's reach into China. There will be a new strategy implemented with a new (increased) budget soon.
>
> Remark: It's pretty awesome how many emails I get from people asking about bitcoin or litecoin or peercoin. It's difficult for me to quantify how much my marketing budget has resulted in introducing crypto currencies to people for the first time. If CB helps to spread the word of this amazing movement, then that's great! And to put things into perspective, if the industry grows to $10 billion in the next couple years and if CB can end up representing 0.1% of the market, then that would equate to CB having a $10 million market cap--CB's current market cap is about $248K. These are exciting times indeed!
>
> Don't forget, the mining subsidy halves in less than a week to 0.6125 (at block 195001).
>
> I'll hopefully have more info about the project releases and marketing budget updates in the not too distant future, but unfortunately I'll have to be cliche and say, stay tuned...
> Cheers. -Merc"

NOVEMBER 2013

On the 6th of November at 17:49:56 UTC, user "elambert" said:

> "Mac client for v 1.1.6.4 available at website now"

Four days later, the fourth halving of the reward attributed to each and every proof of work block occurred. As soon as block number 195,000 had been timestamped, the number of CBX generated stood at 895,483.83496919 CBX.

> Block #195,000 (Reward 1.25 CBX) November 10th 2013 at 01:16:45 PM UTC

> Block #195,001 (Reward 0.625 CBX) November 10th 2013 at 01:18:40 PM UTC

Since the release of version 1.1.6.4 of the wallet client on the 5th of November, users had been having problems downloading the blockchain. One recurring issue concerned reports of a "pop up" which read:

> "WARNING: Checkpoint is too old. Wait for block chain to download, or notify developers."

Another fault was the splash screen staying solely on just before the wallet client finally crashed. This appeared to be the case on certain operating systems.

Loyal supporters of the coin were keen to find out what the next project announcement would be. The developers encouraged patience as announcements would most likely be made during the month. On the 14th of November at 07:38:41 UTC, user "mercSuey" said:

> "I will add another checkpoint soon anyways and build new clients. Probably mid-next week, and that will fix the issues then. In the mean time it doesn't seem serious and I'm in the middle of this project development. And like I said, I haven't noticed issues myself but I'm running Win8 and Ubuntu 12.04."

NOVEMBER 2013

On the 14th of November at 10:13:29 UTC, user "FiniteByDesign" said:

In the middle of November, user "mercSuey" introduced a project he had been working on. Known as the MADEsparq Project, it was described as:

> "This new paradigm, named the MADEsparq Project, aims to blur the defining lines between currency, technology, and data by using the CB block chain to mediate the mapping of data to create, and add value, to content and unstructured and semi-structured data."

However, this project never materialised and would soon be discontinued.

On the 16th of November, the market capitalisation of Crypto Bullion surpassed the $1 million threshold for the first time. The surge had more to do with the fiat increase in Bitcoin than it had to do with the Bitcoin Satoshi rise of CBX.

On the 18th of November, a second Yahoo Finance article was written and published about the coin. Titled "Cryptogenic Bullion—The Virtual Commodity Blurring the Lines Between Currency and Big Data", it described the new major project user "mercSuey" had embarked upon. As can be read in the appendix of this book, the first paragraph of the article is:

> "The lead project developer of Cryptogenic Bullion (CB), Mercury Stills, recently unveiled details of his major project, MADEsparq Project. A white paper has been published on the CB website. From the white paper, "This new paradigm, named the MADEsparq Project, aims to blur the defining lines between currency, technology, and data by using the CB block chain to mediate the mapping of data to create, and add value, to content and unstructured and semi-structured data."

Also on this day, a video games retailer located online at http://bananalizard.com began to accept CBX as a means of payment.

On the 24th of November at 12:51:28 UTC, user "elambert" said:

> "I am noticing more and more individuals getting involved on the CB threads lately, this is great to see! A coin is only as strong as the community that supports and participates in its growth so keep spreading the word and keep those creative juices flowing! Merc has taken an enormous amount on his shoulders and with his new project taking off, community support and development assistance will aid in CB's continued rise to prosperity.
>
> Get involved!"

As the market capitalisation of the coin continued to rise, a wiki site devoted to all things CBX was suggested. User "mercSuey" said it would be a very beneficial site on which information about mining could be easily accessible. He went onto say:

> "A wiki is a great idea and I hope someone can write it up! I would do it myself, but I'm already doing everything and there's only 24 hours in one day."

A few users were happy to contribute to the write up of a wiki site and host it.

NOVEMBER 2013

On the 26th of November at 13:18:03 UTC, user "elambert" said:

> "CB projection/goal for 2013 re-target. I have said since July that my personal goal for CB was 1 CB > 1 LTC by the end of the year (please note that the cost of 1 CB has surpassed the cost of 1 LTC's value at the time of the projection but LTC has increased exponentially as well so technically the goal has not been met). The way crypto's have taken off recently, I thought I would adjust this projection slightly. Although 1 CB > 1 LTC is still a living goal for the year I foresee a smaller goal to be more likely. I would like to go on record predicting CB's market cap to reach $10 million USD by the end of the year. Yes, that means 1 CB > $10 in the next month. Here are my reasons:
>
> 1. Bitcoin boom opening the door for crypto exposure
> 2. MADEsparq
> 3. Closing of MCX combined with Cryptsy's facelift bringing in exponential investors/capital to primary trading platform for CB
> 4. Prospect of getting added to BTC38 where exposure to the Chinese investors will occur
> 5. Continued advertising and community growth and involvement
>
> Again, these are merely my personal goals for CB which I feel are very reachable."

Over the next couple of days leading up to Thanksgiving, the development team, especially user "mercSuey", were working hard to promote Crypto Bullion as a unique and innovative cryptocurrency. They wanted to make the coin as distinctive as possible; not be perceived as another cloned cryptocurrency.

On the 28th of November at 11:23:35 UTC, user "elambert" said:

> "Happy Thanksgiving to the whole CB community! It has been a wild ride this past 5 months and I am truly thankful for the experience and the participation of the whole community. We have come so far in this short time together and this is just the beginning! I hope everyone who celebrates today has an opportunity to put crypto aside for the day and spend some quality time with their loved ones, remember, that is what this life experience is about. Enjoy, eat, drink, laugh and love! Catch your breath and get refreshed, I suspect a parabola in the future"

NOVEMBER 2013

On the 30th of November at 11:53:45 UTC, user "FiniteByDesign" said:

"Physical Cryptogenic Bullion bars made from 1 troy ounce of .999 fine silver are in! I will be having professional photos done soon but here are a couple snapshots for the time being."

As the month came to a close, user "mercSuey" was overwhelmed by how many e-mails he was receiving. He was confident people were beginning to discover the true value and unique potential of Crypto Bullion.

Crypto Bullion—History of the First Year

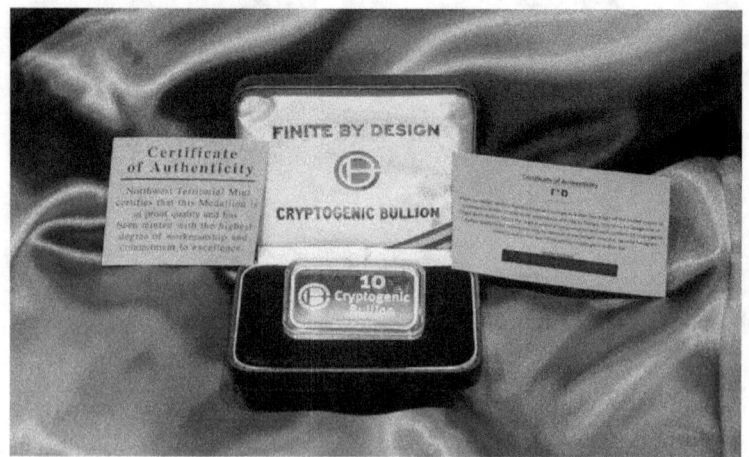

ALL TIME HIGH MARKET CAPITALISATION OF CRYPTO BULLION ATTAINED
DECEMBER 2013

I. All time high market capitalisation of about $5,663,750 attained.

II. Some translations of the official website were inadequate.

III. Cryptsy initiated live direct trading between Crypto Bullion and Litecoin.

IV. PoW block reward halved from 0.625 CBX to 0.3125 CBX.

V. Crypto card paper wallets made available by FiniteByDesign.

On the 1st of December, the market capitalisation of CBX reached an all time high of ~$5,663,750 according to historical charts from www.coinmarketcap.com. Also on this website, it states the Bitcoin value of one unit of CBX account at this peak as 0.00574388 BTC. According to www.cryptocoincharts.info, the recorded Bitcoin Satoshi trading values (Cryptsy) on this day were:

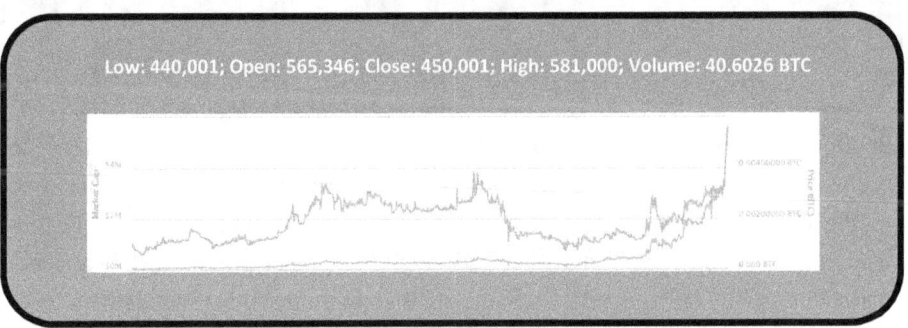

Low: 440,001; Open: 565,346; Close: 450,001; High: 581,000; Volume: 40.6026 BTC

Discussion resumed about Crypto Bullion possibly being added to further exchanges. On the 3rd of December at 00:18:39 UTC, user "mercSuey" said:

> "I already emailed them...they have QQ email info at the bottom of their site. They are extremely busy with customer support emails from their users.
>
> Note, btc38 is fueled by speculators and wild price changes. Just look at MEC, in the last four days it reached over 18 CNY to a low of 5 CNY today (72% loss), settling at around 8 CNY currently.
>
> I'd be excited to see CB trading on btc38, but there are positives to not being traded on there as well. CB needs stable and steady adoption, not wild price swings that can scare away legitimate business usage.
>
> I'm working on getting CB on more exchanges, but that's just my two satoshi..."

Also on this day, an announcement was made that the official Crypto Bullion website at http://cryptogenicbullion.org was, at this time, available to view in nine different languages. However, someone noticed the Swedish translation was not professional and had clearly been translated using "Google Translator". Word for word, user "110110101" said:

> "As a native English/Swedish speaker I must inform you that the Swedish translation appears to be a Google-translation at best, or just painfully incorrect at worst. It is so bad that you might want to consider having the Swedish part offline until it is rewritten.
>
> If needed, I could try to find time to help out, but I can only put in a little time here and there. Too much to do between family, work and rebuilding our house. That said, let me know if I can help the CGB community!"

Bounties were offered to user "110110101" and anyone else who was willing to professionally translate the content of the official website. Other translations such as the German and Turkish versions were also awful. In order to avoid further inadequate versions, user "mercSuey" decided to go ahead with hiring professional translators, with real credentials, who would then be sufficiently rewarded.

On the 7th of December, user "mercSuey" received some valuable marketing input for the official website. As a result, he used this to change the text content there. He described these changes as follows:

> "The changes I've made express CB to be a universal commodity and not seemingly just for business needs. A universal commodity/currency is more accurate anyways and the literature on the website should properly express it.
>
> I've also added a couple more paragraphs in the About section regarding being more environmentally friendly than strictly proof of work coins as well as unique project development initiatives which very few other coins can even begin to claim."

Two days later, user "mercSuey" said a brand new wallet client, version 2.0, was scheduled to be released in February or March 2014. He emphasised this was only a tentative timescale due to all the other projects (MADEsparq) he was working on. An Android wallet was also scheduled to coincide with the 2.0 wallet release.

Also on the 9th of December, user "mercSuey" mentioned a potential design contest to design a logo for the MADEsparq Project. Before this, he wanted get the "initial functionality" finished for the project.

On the 12th of December at 09:46:07 UTC, user "elambert" said:

> "A few updates for the community:
>
> - Mercury has added additional download options for the CB client for those that cannot access Google links: https://cryptogenicbullion.org/#download
>
> - CB appears to be on the shortlist for addition at BTC38: http://www.btc38.com/altcoin/
>
> - CB PoW subsidy will be halving in about 3 days from .625 to .3125 reward per block. So in about 3 days, the daily minting of CB via PoW will decrease from 900 CB per day to 450 CB per day: http://explorer.cryptogenicbullion.org:2750/chain/CryptogenicBullion"

DECEMBER 2013

On the 14th of December, direct trading between Crypto Bullion and Litecoin went live on the Cryptsy exchange platform. This was 208 days after the launch of the exchange. This exchange ceased operations on the 14th of January 2016 (see page 43 for further information).

On the following day, the fifth halving of the reward attributed to each proof of work block occurred. As soon as block number 245,000 had been timestamped, the number of CBX generated stood at 921,438.55980619 CBX.

Block #245,000 (Reward 0.625 CBX) December 15th 2013 at 03:44:05 PM UTC

Block #245,001 (Reward 0.3125 CBX) December 15th 2013 at 03:44:33 PM UTC

On the 19th of December at 10:41:04 UTC, user "FiniteByDesign" said:

"Finite By Design's Crypto Card (paper wallets) available now!

https://bitcointalk.org/index.php?topic=377130.msg4039766#msg4039766

Here are a couple of images, I will be adding professional ones in the coming days:

DECEMBER 2013

User "mercSuey" appreciated the manufacture of these paper wallets. He relayed the message to interested members of the community.

On the 27th of December at 19:26:50 UTC, user "elambert" said:

> "BTW, for those using Cryptsy, please note they have added 2-factor authentication via Authy (mobile app). I have used this with Coinbase for some time and love it. I would encourage those with holdings at Cryptsy to take advantage of this new feature."

It was a common view held by many to keep one's coins as secure as possible.

On the penultimate day of December, an article was published on the website at http://www.businessinsider.com.au/ titled "There Are Now At Least 14 Digital Currencies Worth More Than $US1". Written by Rob Wile, he had retrieved the data from the site www.coinmarketcap.com. In descending order, these were:

> Bitcoin: ~$800 (Mt. Gox price)
> Mastercoin: $US180.25
> Bitbar: $US44
> Litecoin: $US24.15
> Protoshares: $US19.59
> Novacoin: $US13.72
> Unobtanium: $US6.30
> Namecoin: $US5
> Anoncoin: $US4.61
> Peercoin: $US4.28
> Primecoin: $US2.68
> Franko: $US2.31
> Cryptogenic Bullion: $US2.21
> Diamond: $US2.20

By the end of 2013, there had been 928,438.79785819 CBX generated.

> Block #268,311 (Reward 0.3125 CBX) December 31st 2013 at 11:59:07 PM UTC

83

NEW PLANS FOR CRYPTO BULLION IN 2014
JANUARY 2014

I. What is your favourite characteristic of Crypto Bullion?

II. Version 1.1.6.5 of the wallet client released.

III. PoW block reward halved from 0.3125 CBX to 0.15625 CBX.

IV. FiniteByDesign one gram silver crypto card prototype produced.

V. A new official website coming soon...

On the original Crypto Bullion Bitcointalk thread, user "elambert" submitted the first post of 2014. As a means to celebrate the new year, he encouraged people to post their favourite characteristic of Crypto Bullion, as well as their wallet address, on that thread. They would then each receive 0.1 CBX (aka. a thread faucet of coins). Aspects of the coin which people liked were:

- Proof of work/stake hybrid as the timestamping algorithm;
- A very rare and scarce number of coins in circulation;
- A great name referring to value and security;
- A very active and committed development team.

Other qualities mentioned by the community related to the sixty second block time, the relative price stability and the inherent interest rate on coins held in the wallet.

JANUARY 2014

On the 7th of January at 00:16:45 UTC, user "elambert" said:

> "New client released, 1.1.6.5, new team members announced and message from lead dev, Mercury Stills!
>
> https://cryptogenicbullion.org/#blog"

Versions for Windows and Linux were now available for download. User "maxpower" was working on the Mac OS X version.

On the same day at 20:16:27 UTC, user "FiniteByDesign" said:

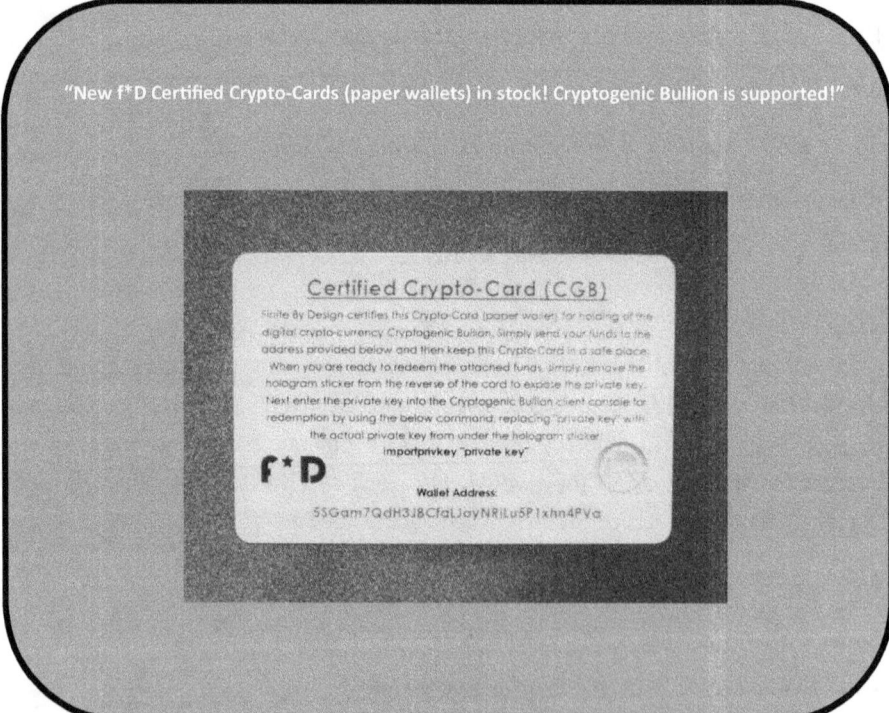

On the following day, courtesy of user "maxpower", the Mac OS X wallet client (version 1.1.6.5) was successfully released. A few hours later, the corresponding download link was posted on the official Crypto Bullion Bitcointalk thread.

JANUARY 2014

On the 15th of January, user "RandomUser456" enquired if there was a concrete plan ahead for the year 2014. He was concerned about the recent fall in value of the market capitalisation since the all time high on the 1st of December 2013. He wanted to know whether any new updates were planned in the near future. By releasing regular updates, he thought this would sustain strong interest in the coin. In response, user "elambert" said:

> "Yes, there are plans for CB in 2014. As you mentioned, MADEsparq is in development. Additionally we have expanded the CB team and we are prioritizing our projects and marketing plans. We will continue to share with the community as much as possible and as often as possible. Stay tuned."

Despite the fall in value of the coin, there were some people who saw this a positive in the long run. User "Killiz" viewed it as a great opportunity to buy Crypto Bullion at cheaper rate. He congratulated the development team on releasing promised updates punctually and professionally. He also understood how devoted the team and community were to building a solid infrastructure around the coin.

On the 16th of January at 19:48:09 UTC, user "mercSuey" said:

> "Congrats to http://coinpayments.net for winning CB's 2013 Partnership Award.
>
> Also congrats to http://www.multipool.us and http://finitebydesign.net for winning Honorable Mention.
>
> First announced on the dev blog: https://cryptogenicbullion.org/#blog"

As mentioned in the quote directly above, www.coinpayments.net had been rewarded $300 for winning the "CB 2013 Partnership Award". It is a site which allows individuals and business to incorporate a means by which they can buy/sell their goods/services using cryptocurrency.

JANUARY 2014

On the 19th of January at 19:58:59 UTC, user "elambert" announced the following:

> "PoW subsidy is now 0.15625 CGB per block! Only 225 new CGB minted each day! But don't worry, you can buy them @https://www.cryptsy.com/markets/view/70"

This was the sixth halving of the proof of work mining block reward:

> Block #295,000 (Reward 0.3125 CBX) January 19th 2014 at 04:10:00 PM UTC

> Block #295,001 (Reward 0.15625 CBX) January 19th 2014 at 04:12:29 PM UTC

Three days later, user "BitcoinFX" published a photo (see page 84) of a first draft mock-up Cryptogenic Bullion card concept he had been working on. They were being designed as collectible gifts to be sold by FiniteByDesign. As shown in the image, each laminated card held one gram of sterling silver. Other versions holding one gram of 9ct gold, 18ct gold and platinum were scheduled to be produced too.

On the 25th of January, user "Dragoon" wanted to know if any progress had been made to get Crypto Bullion on exchanges such as BTC-e or Vircurex. On this day at 13:24:05 UTC, user "elambert" responded by saying:

> "We continue to send communications but nothing definitive that I have heard. We also continue to reach out to other exchanges. The community can definitely help by submitting requests to their choice exchanges.
>
> Also we are working on growing the community so any social media support is welcomed. Some coins have numerous twitter accounts posting coin specific things, news, price, etc. CB has one that I run but others would certainly help to spread the word of CB.
>
> CGB stands out for those in the know as an alternative to the clone war/max-minting crypto-currencies as it is a scarce - storage of wealth - interest bearing crypto-commodity. CGB is one of a kind in a watered down landscape. Lets continue to spread the word and bring as many people along for the ride as possible!"

JANUARY 2014

On the 26th of January at 01:52:51 UTC, user "mercSuey" said:

> "Marketing is ongoing with Facebook clicks and Google Adwords at about $500/month out of my pocket.
>
> It was effective at first and CB was a top ten coin for awhile but has fallen out of favor for the most recent fad of animal coins and planet coins (lol).
>
> Given the obvious fickleness of the crowd and network effect, I doubt marketing will have any resounding effect at this point. Only development results and the expectation of a growing network effect and ecosystem.
>
> I have decided to spend less time on the forums recently because I'd rather spend my time researching/developing. Plus, I admit I'm a bit annoyed/disillusioned of how nonsense scrypt coins based on animals/planets/whatever catch fire and are instantly added to exchanges like Vircurex...it's 'funny' for lack of a better term.
>
> And greed is infecting all kinds of projects now, like Zerocoin, which the heads of the project announced they will release their own coin with zerocoin anonymity built in from the start. And the head developer said something like "If people will put their money into DogeCoins then they'll put their money into anything..."
>
> But CB is a community project like any other crypto currency. And everyone's contribution will add to the CB network effect and ecosystem. And regardless of being named after animals or planets or whatever, if the network effect is there then there is value. So I can belittle this whole DogeCoin nonsense all I want but the fact is that its network is huge already.
>
> Like I said on my Twitter feed, all I can do is just keep grinding along and eventually things will sort themselves out."

The response above by user "mercSuey" was directed towards somebody who was disappointed they had lost money due to the recent fall in the fiat value of CBX (they bought CBX at approximately $3 per CBX unit).

User "mercSuey" also commented on the cards "BitcoinFX" was designing, promoting and producing. He described the silver version as gorgeous and looked forward to its release. He also reiterated the fact that development was ongoing. All future updates would be published on the official CBX Blog (as had been the case for several weeks). Progress was acknowledged as slow, but worth the wait.

JANUARY 2014

On the 29th of January, user "mercSuey" made the community aware that any coin giveaways on Bitcointalk had to be discontinued. This forum had decided to ban users from participating in this process. To be trivial, user "Trail48" was the last known user to receive CBX via an official coin giveaway. Periodic future giveaways were promised on other social media sites such as Facebook and Twitter.

On the 30th of January at 10:50:13 UTC, user "elambert" posted:

> "Due to the constant state of flux in the crypto landscape, we must be flexible and continue to adapt and change the priority of projects as necessary so it is difficult to give concrete milestones and timelines. The main focal points however for 2014 are: technical development and community growth. Those in the community such as yourself can help tremendously in the area of community growth by spreading the word of CGB and its differentiation that makes it something special - i.e. social media, chat rooms, merchants, videos, forums, technical write up guides, exchange requests, etc.
>
> Should you have particular technical skills and ideas that you think would be beneficial to CGB's community and success, please feel free to contact us via the website to discuss. We are currently a team of 3 with a 4th potential member in an evaluation stage as we speak so we continue to grow our manpower to address all of the lofty plans that we have and continue to dream up. Here are a few of the specific projects that are in development now:
>
> 1. MADEsparq
> 2. New website
> 3. Additional translations
> 4. CGB dedicated forum
> 5. CGB client 2.0
> 6. Continued push for addition to exchanges
> 7. Growth of the CGB community and development team
> 8. Advertising, advertising, advertising
>
> Additional details and projects will be revealed in time but lets just say there is a lot being done in the background.
>
> Thank you for your support and offer to assist; community adoption, ownership and responsibility for CGB are in my opinion critical to CGB's success. You can see everyday more and more people getting a stake and getting involved. The current price-point is a delicious entry invitation and of course all are welcomed with open arms. We are all very excited about the projects and developments in the pipeline and look forward to working in tandem with the community."

JANUARY 2014

Other events which occurred in the month of January were:

- On the 3rd of January, a health supplement and detox company at http://citrusfit.com began to accept Crypto Bullion as a means of payment.

- On the 9th of January, an exchange called OpenEx began to offer active trading of CBX at https://openex.pw/index.php?page=trade&market=5. Five days later, user "elambert" politely requested users to withdraw their CBX from there after seeing an official announcement by OpenEx to do so.

- A website at http://www.mintagemastermind.com began to accept CBX in exchange for precious metals on the 22nd of January.

91

DIRECTOR OF MARKETING AND STRATEGY USER "PAPERSHEEPDOG" JOINED THE CBX TEAM

FEBRUARY 2014

I. An exchange called Cryptokopen initated live trading of Crypto Bullion.

II. First post on the official CBX Bitcointalk thread by user "papersheepdog".

III. Tipping of Crypto Bullion on Reddit was initiated by user "artiface".

IV. Gold themed Crypto Bullion graphics designed and published.

V. PoW block reward halved from 0.15625 CBX to 0.078125 CBX.

On the 1st of February at 22:58:53 UTC, user "elambert" announced that Crypto Bullion had recently been added to its sixth exchange trading platform. Trading here no longer exists:

FEBRUARY 2014

On the 3rd of February at 18:11:18 UTC, user "papersheepdog" posted his first comment on the original Crypto Bullion Bitcointalk thread:

> "Hi Guys, I am new to the community but very impressed with CGB. I have created the above image and am trying to get some community excitement happening on Reddit over at http://www.reddit.com/r/CryptogenicBullion/. Please let me know what you think of the image (feel free to share) and join us on Reddit as a presence is needed here to really push this amazing opportunity.
>
> Regards, Papersheepdog"

He was referring to image as shown at the top of page 92. There were a few criticisms, but user "elambert" loved the image. He sent 10 CBX to him as thanks.

On the 4th of February at 22:24:40 UTC, user "BitcoinFX" said:

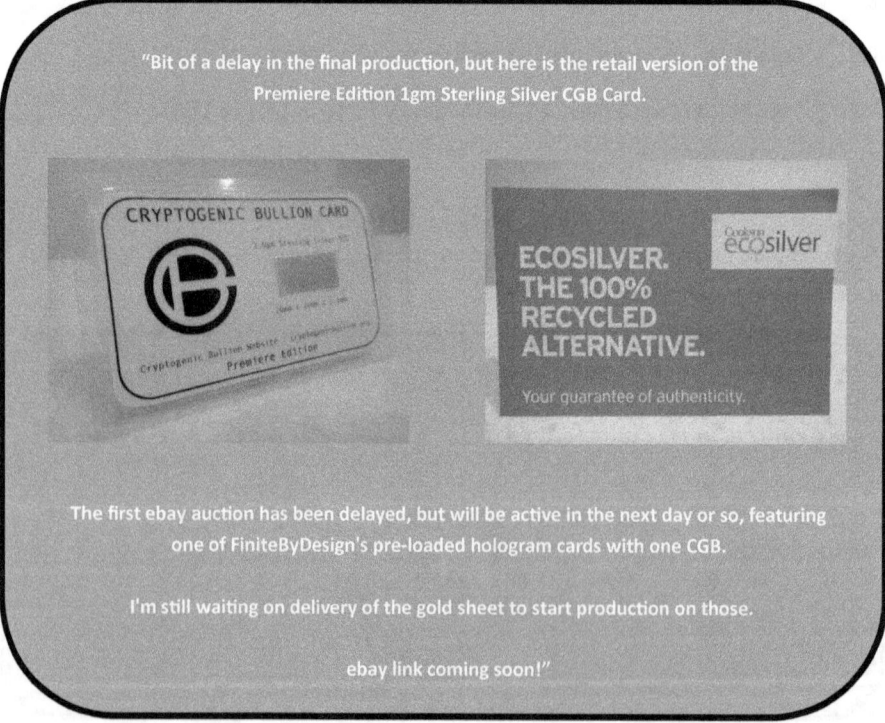

> "Bit of a delay in the final production, but here is the retail version of the Premiere Edition 1gm Sterling Silver CGB Card.
>
> The first ebay auction has been delayed, but will be active in the next day or so, featuring one of FiniteByDesign's pre-loaded hologram cards with one CGB.
>
> I'm still waiting on delivery of the gold sheet to start production on those.
>
> ebay link coming soon!"

On the following day, a lighter redesign of the official website went live (see the bottom of page 91). Somebody known by the name "Ben" was responsible for the change, despite user "mercSuey" being in charge of the website. The main purpose was to make it look more simple and easier to navigate. It was not long before members of the community began to criticise the lighter version. This had also been the case with the darker version (see below). User "mercSuey" understood and acknowledged the concerns from both sides. If a resounding number of people wanted to revert back to the darker version, they were willing to so.

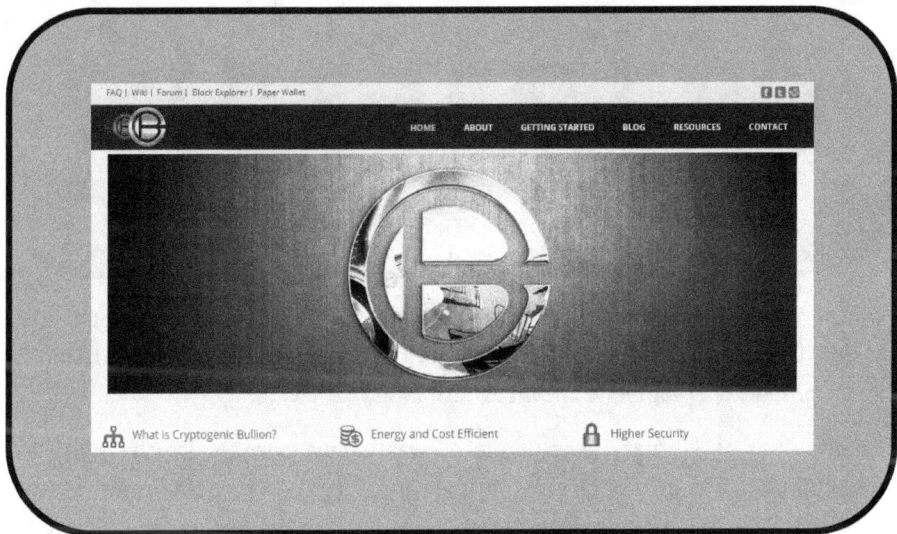

On the same day, the website design did revert to the darker version. After much thought and opinions from the community, user "mercSuey" thought the colour scheme of the lighter version was not an improvement and too simple. As a first impression, it was deterring visitors straight away. Someone went as far to say it looked like the site was from 2002. User "mercSuey" wanted the new site, whenever it may be released, to be "jaw dropping awesome", both visually and practically. He had faith in Ben working on it until it reached that level.

On the 9th of February, the presentational theme and colours of the official Crypto Bullion Subreddit at http://www.reddit.com/r/CryptogenicBullion were changed. Thanks were given to "/u/igl00FTW" who contributed greatly to it.

FEBRUARY 2014

On the 9th of February at 09:35:42 UTC, user "papersheepdog" posted:

> "Check it 😊
>
> CGB on Reddit:
> http://www.reddit.com/r/CryptogenicBullion
>
> CGB Marketing Campaign Headquarters:
> http://www.reddit.com/r/GotCrypto/
>
> CGB - Open Source Community Development and Marketing Strategy (Master Document):
> http://www.reddit.com/r/GotCrypto/comments/1x7j2w/
> cgb_open_source_community_development_and/
>
> Community on Reddit at /r/CryptoMarkets - First highlighted community:
> http://www.reddit.com/r/GotCrypto/comments/1xf923/
> highlighted_community_on_reddit_at_rcryptomarkets/"

On the following day, the first promotional video for Crypto Bullion was uploaded to YouTube. Titled "Cryptogenic Bullion - Crypto Currency - Run with the BULLion!", it was produced by someone known as "CGfanBoy".

On the 16th of February, user "artiface" was happy to announce that the CBX Reddit TipBot was in testing phase in the /r/GotCrypto subreddit. Once he was confident of everything working properly, he would then expand the TipBot to other subreddits including http://www.reddit.com/r/CryptogenicBullion.

Three days later at 03:29:20 UTC, user "artiface" was quoted as saying:

> "The reddit GotCrypto tip bot seems to be working well. I have enabled it for the /r/CryptoGenicbullion subreddit."

On the 20th of February, a new exchange called Comkort went live. Traders of Crypto Bullion would have to wait until the 27th of April 2014 for the addition of CBX on their trading platform.

On the official CBX Subreddit, user "scriib" published several "Gold Themed" CBX coin logo/graphics. On the 20th of February at 17:47:28 UTC, he said:

> "Alright guys, I've started working on a gold theme for CGB so I thought I'd post up some designs for feedback/suggestions. So far rendered them a slightly dull gold colour, thinking could try a shinier version. Opinions appreciated ;)"
>
> MULTIPLY THE VALUE OF YOUR BITCOINS WITH CRYPTOGENIC BULLION
>
> Cryptogenic Bullion ACCEPTED HERE
>
> http://www.reddit.com/r/CryptogenicBullion/comments/1yggws/gold_cgb_theme/

Special thanks were given to users "Cryptasm" and "redphelm" for the above graphics and new slogan. Somebody loved that they were not genuinely gold, only slightly golden. In particular, user "papersheepdog" said:

> I love the subtlety! In your face shiny gold is overplayed and unsophisticated. This is seriously cool."

> Block #345,000 (Reward 0.15625 CBX) February 23rd 2014 at 04:37:28 PM UTC

> Block #345,001 (Reward 0.078125 CBX) February 23rd 2014 at 04:38:41 PM UTC

On the 23rd of February, the seventh halving of the reward attributed to each and every proof of work block occurred. As soon as block number 345,000 had been timestamped, the number of CBX generated stood at 943,559.12679919 CBX.

As shown below, the Bitcoin Satoshi values of one unit of CBX account on Cryptsy were as follows:

	Price	Low	Open	Close	High	Volume (BTC)
24th of Feb	116,081	100,000	120,675	111,487	122,998	14.2077
25th of Feb	104,019	90,000	111,487	96,551	111,488	11.7696
26th of Feb	95,853	78,892	96,546	95,160	101,359	27.0277
27th of Feb	85,079.5	75,000	95,159	75,000	96,119	12.2776
28th of Feb	80,502.5	76,480	79,002	82,003	85,201	4.89354

source: www.cryptocoincharts.info

User "elambert" was puzzled to witness the steep decline in the Bitcoin Satoshi value. By remaining positive, he viewed it as beneficial to all those traders and recipient buyers who had had their buy orders filled. Despite the disappointing decrease in Bitcoin Satoshi value, there was strong optimism throughout the community. According to the opinion of user "elambert", he had never seen the community more actively involved. He was happy to see talented and dedicated individuals helping to push the coin towards a sustained long term objective.

Discussion had begun to shift to Reddit during the month. User "elambert" emphasised the importance of keeping the official Crypto Bullion Bitcointalk thread updated with any news posted at www.reddit.com/r/CryptogenicBullion/.

As the month came to a close, efforts were continuing to get Crypto Bullion noticed by more cryptocurrency exchanges. One of these potential exchanges was called MintPal (no longer active). Members of the community were being encouraged to vote six times per hour (if registered) or three times per hour (if not registered). Poloniex and BTC38 were also being sought after as potential trading platforms for the coin. Six exchanges had initiated CBX live trading since the launch of the coin.

Other events which occurred in the month of February were:

- On the 9th of February, user "x0rcist" announced the release of the online paper wallet generator at https://cgbaddress.org. However, he did advise initial caution as additional testing was required. He recommended users to experiment with small amounts of CBX first. This site is no longer available. User "elambert" appreciated his work and offered to send him some CBX. User "x0rcist" declined to accept some by saying it was a gift to the community.
- Throughout most of the month, ten votes per day were permitted at http://www.allcrypt.com/beta/voting.php. Also, voting to get CBX added to Ecoinfund and Bter (two Chinese exchanges) was encouraged.
- On the 20th of February, a new slogan to accompany the recently designed gold/silver coin logo was published (see page 100).
- On 22nd of February, CBX was added to www.bluecoinstock.com. This was a site on which users were able to have their own dashboard charting all their coins. A total US Dollar valuation of their coin portfolio was visible.
- On the 24th of February, the total number of subscribers on the official CBX Subreddit at www.reddit.com/r/CryptogenicBullion surpassed 100.
- On the 27th February, the online merchandiser FiniteByDesign added gold CBX crypto cards, alongside the silver equivalent, to their available stock.

CRYPTOGENIC BULLION

EARN. STORE. MULTIPLY.

LEAD DEVELOPER RESIGNED AND FOUR EXCHANGES INITIATED CBX TRADING

MARCH 2014

I. User "mercSuey" resigned from the core development team.

II. Version 1.1.6.6 of the wallet client released.

III. New official website went live at http://cgb.holdings.

IV. An exchange called Bittrex initiated live trading of the coin.

V. PoW block reward halved from 0.078125 CBX to 0.039062 CBX.

Most trading of CBX was occurring on Cryptsy. On this exchange, the value of one unit of CBX account had continued to fall until it descended to a low of 21,090 Bitcoin Satoshi on the 1st of March. This value turned out to be the lowest Bitcoin Satoshi figure recorded on that exchange for the entire first year history of Crypto Bullion. Also on this day, there was further disappointing news regarding the development team. At 13:43:49 UTC, user "elambert" announced:

> "I just received an email from Mercury stating he has resigned from the CGB development team in order to focus on other projects. My apologies to the community as this was not expected and has caught me unprepared. Good news, I think the dumping should subside now. Bad news, it will take a little time to build the development team. The lead dev position is the immediate concern and will be my focus to resolve as soon as possible. Again, my apologies to the community. We will rebound and be better than before."

MARCH 2014

Confidence in the future of the coin had been shaken. A significant number of people were beginning to give up on Crypto Bullion after seeing their investment decrease in value. They were also unhappy with the way in which user "mercSuey" had abruptly left (and sold his stake). Therefore, there was no chance of there being a smooth transition to fill the vacant lead developer position. Needless to say, praise was due for his prior enthusiasm and dedication to the coin. Taking immediate effect, Crypto Bullion was no longer affiliated with the MADEsparq Project.

Despite the disappointing news, the development team and wider community viewed this as an opportunity. A "re-birth" of the coin was encouraged. Taking into account that user "mercSuey" was in control of http://cryptogenicbullion.org (founded on the 10th of August 2013), a new website was called for. In the interim, the official Crypto Bullion Subreddit acted as the coin's home.

On the 1st of March at 18:19:43 UTC, user "elambert" was quoted as saying:

> "It is with great pleasure that I would like to announce the new lead developer of Cryptogenic Bullion, Artiface! Artiface has been active for some time in the CGB community and brings with him an impressive resume as a software engineer. Additional to his undertakings outside of the crypto world, he is the creator of the CGB tipbot currently deployed on Reddit.
>
> This appointment is by no means a step down from the previous developer. Certainly there are some large shoes to fill but I am confident that Artiface is the right individual for this job. Please join me in welcoming Artiface and showing him some love and support! His first order of business is to update checkpoints, handle a long overdue fix between the getbalance and listaccounts showing a discrepancy and to update the splash screen logo with our new Gold theme and new slogan "Earn. Store. Multiply.".
>
> I have another development team addition announcement to make soon and also have extended offers to some of the core community members to also join the team in an official capacity.
>
> Please keep in mind that this is still a community project and the development team works on a volunteer basis for the community and also to add value to their personal stake. If you want to get involved, this is a great time to acquire stake at a discount and join in to help launch Cryptogenic Bullion to the next level!"

Roughly half an hour later, user "artiface" introduced himself as the new lead developer of Crypto Bullion. He was quoted as saying:

> "Thanks elambert!
>
> This is a great coin and a great community and I am honored to be added to the development team. Just so everyone knows a bit of my background I am a professional software engineer, with 10+ years industry experience and 20+ years of programming experience. I currently have a role as lead developer of a multi-million dollar industrial product line. I have also made fixes and contributions to several other coin projects. I am confident that I have the experience and ability to take on this role.
>
> I am working right now to get the development environment ready. I hope to have a new client version available within the week.
>
> Thanks to this great community, I have high hopes for the future of CGB!"

As described by user "elambert", the last twenty four hours had been turbulent and had caught him off guard. A new development team was being assembled.

On the 4th of March, user "papersheepdog" published a "CGB Core Team Meeting Update" in which he listed members in the newly formed core development team. This team consisted of seven people:

> Elambert – Founder, Leader
> Artiface – Lead Developer
> papersheepdog – Director of Marketing and Strategy
> x0rcist – Core Team Member
> Killiz – Core Team Member
> Ethapus – Core Team Member
> (non-public) – Core Team Member

Additionally, both a temporary official website at http://www.gotcrypto.net and block explorer at http://blocks.gotcrypto.net/chain/CryptogenicBullion were established. An arrangement to have the previous domain of the official website transferred back to the community was ongoing. This never materialised.

MARCH 2014

On the 8th of March at 18:12:16 UTC, user "elambert" said:

> "It is with great pleasure that I announce the most recent updates from the Cryptogenic Bullion development team! Client Version 1.1.6.6:
>
> - Updated splash screen; Updated logos; Updated checkpoints
> - Fix to getbalance vs listaccounts discrepancy
>
> ...(DOWNLOAD LINK)...
>
> Stay tuned!"

Besides the announcement immediately above, user "elambert" was happy to make the community aware of the next wallet client release. To be released as version 1.1.6.7, it was scheduled to be available for download within the next month. A sample set of features to be included in this version were stated:

- Visualisation of PoS staking and estimated time until next reward.
- Button for unlocking wallet to stake instead of having to go through the console.
- Update checkpointing code.

On the 10th of March, the seventh exchange initiated active trading of CBX. AllCrypt was announced on the 29th of January 2014 and, six days later, began to permit people to vote for their favourite coins for addition. It went live on the 28th of February, but no longer exists. User "bahamapascal" posted:

> "CryptogenicBullion is now trading on AllCrypt.com!!!!
> Good job every one for all your voting, thanks to your awesome support we made it.
>
> https://www.allcrypt.com/market?id=212"

After a hack and theft of ~42 BTC, it closed operations on the 16th of March 2015.

MARCH 2014

On the 11th of March, user "papersheepdog" published a "CGB Core Team Weekly Update" in which he informed the community of the goals and directions being worked on. After the most recent client release, priority shifted towards the new upcoming official website. User "papersheepdog" went onto say the following:

> "We understand that as so much has changed in the CGB community and project, that the website is needed to clarify our new direction. It will provide a rock solid foundation for investors of all backgrounds to understand the true value of CGB and the crypto-markets as a whole. There is a lot of work to be done on this but we believe that we can get a solid site out by the weekend and continue to iron out the finishing touches thereafter."

As well as the efforts being made above, he found time to give special thanks to users "bahamapascal" and "BTCat". They tirelessly promoted and encouraged people to vote for the addition of CBX to AllCrypt. On the same day at 10:22:29 UTC, user "elambert" posted the following on the official CBX Reddit Page:

> "Guys, I did a little testing with AllCrypt.com and I must say I am extremely impressed. I tested deposit and withdrawal and it was almost instantaneous. I did some testing of placing orders and removing orders and this also proved to be quick and easy. I reached out to support and got a response that was helpful, professional and kind. They also provide some very cool features: 1. favourite market selection 2. BTC, LTC and DOGE pairings 3. priority order slection 4. stop order. The only downside is low volume at this time but I am sure this will schange as more people try their service. Needless to say, I am impressed and will continue to use their platform."

On the 17th of March, user "papersheepdog" posted a quick update about the new upcoming official CBX website. Theme customisations were complete and they were working on the layout and text content of each individual page.

MARCH 2014

After two weeks of hard work by the core development team and two months of participation from the community, the new official website went live. On the official CBX Twitter Page, the following was tweeted on the 19th of March:

> "New website cgb.holdings is live!!"

This was ample opportunity for Crypto Billion to move into a new phase of marketing and development. A shift from miners to investors was occurring with the new official website conveying a fresh vision. The vast majority of comments in relation to the newly released official website were positive. Users described it as professional and smart.

On the 23rd of March at 10:16:01 UTC, user "elambert" announced the latest cryptocurrency exchange to add Crypto Bullion:

"Cryptogenic Bullion now trading at Bittrex.com!

https://bittrex.com/Market/Index?MarketName=BTC-CGB"

Members of the community had been able to vote for CBX inclusion there since the 3rd of March 2014 via a Bitcointalk thread. It began trading operations (beta phase) on the 13th of February 2014 and went fully live with 12 coins/21 trading pairs fifteen days later. Based in Seattle, Washington, USA, it is still in operation as one of the major altcoin exchanges alongside Poloniex and BTC-e.

MARCH 2014

On the following day, the first Chinese exchange called Ecoinfund added Crypto Bullion to its trading platform at http://www.ecoinfund.com/market=47. This was welcomed news as it would help to build exposure in Asia.

There had been a recent surge in the number of cryptocurrency exchanges which had become operational. Voting was underway to get Crypto Bullion on other ones including C-Cex, Comkort and MintPal. In particular, the CBX team were happy to announce trading would soon commence on Vault of Satoshi, a Canadian based platform. This would allow direct trades between USD/CAD and CBX for the first time.

On the penultimate day of March, the reward of each proof of work block halved for the eighth time:

Block #395,000 (Reward 0.078125 CBX) March 30th 2014 at 04:03:54 PM UTC

Block #395,001 (Reward 0.039062 CBX) March 30th 2014 at 04:03:56 PM UTC

Other events which occurred in the month of March were:

- On the 5th of March, the second promotional video for Crypto Bullion was uploaded to YouTube by Dennis Saunders. It was simply titled "Cryptogenic Bullion" and ran for thirty seconds. It was created at www.animoto.com.

- On the 23rd of March, voting began at https://c-cex.com/Index.html?id=vote to get CBX on the exchange called C-Cex. At this time, daily trading volume on this platform was relatively low.

- Also on the 23rd of March, prizes for a "Viral Image Contest" were announced. First prize went to Reddit user "/u/magalhanze" for his image (see the top of page 108). He received 60 CBX.

- CBX was added to the exchange called Swaphole on the 28th of March. Other cryptocurrencies such as Bitcoin, Litecoin, Dogecoin and Darkcoin (now known as Dash) were also active on the same day.

DIRECT FIAT TO CBX TRADING MADE AVAILABLE BY VAULT OF SATOSHI

APRIL 2014

I. Version 1.1.6.6 of the wallet client released.

II. Vault of Satoshi initiated direct USD/CAD to CBX trading

III. An exchange called Comkort initiated live trading of Crypto Bullion.

IV. First prize of the "News Beat" contest went to user "paulmaritz".

V. More than half of blocks timestamped to the blockchain were now PoS.

Progress was being made on the next wallet client update, the official website and the continued active presence on Reddit. There was also discussion attaining to whether it would be beneficial to change the coin specification to encourage a even greater proportion of proof of stakes blocks. On the 2nd of April at 09:53:28 UTC, user "elambert" was quoted as saying:

> "One thing I would like to be careful to highlight is that these changes would NOT affect inflation. The 0.5% inflation through PoW mining would remain despite a reward increase of 10x because the generation time would equally multiply by 10x. Also the coin age of 90 days to earn 1.5% annually would remain in tact. The min age of 30 days to earn 1.2% annual interest would be superseded by a min age of 1 day to earn 1% annual interest. Again, this daily min age for staking would populate the network with more PoS blocks to both speed the transaction time and better secure the network."

APRIL 2014

Also on the 1st of April, the value of one unit of CBX account surpassed 100,000 Bitcoin Satoshi again on Cryptsy. The last time it was above this level was on the 26th of February 2014 (a high on Cryptsy of 101,359 BTC Satoshi).

	Price	Low	Open	Close	High	Volume (BTC)
1st of April	85,182	74,275	74,275	96,085	130,000	21.8288
2nd of April	100,567.5	90,000	98,387	102,745	130,333	10.5183
3rd of April	106,884	99,138	102,759	111.009	126,000	14.6093
4th of April	110,273.5	105,500	109,520	111,027	115,349	3.11558
5th of April	109,498.5	100,000	113,998	104,999	113,998	4.12439
6th of April	105,175.5	102,351	102,351	108,000	108,000	2.22465
7th of April	110,708.5	105,050	108,000	113,417	130,739	7.11011
8th of April	123,653	114,126	124,758	122,548	135,181	4.08085

source: www.cryptocoincharts.info

As is true at the time of publication, the high on the 8th of April has not been reached or surpassed ever since.

Taking into account how lacklustre the translations of the original official website were in 2013, a renewed effort was underway to translate the content of http://cgb.holdings. On the 7th of April, the CBX Team called for help from bilingual supporters of the coin. Chinese and Japanese were significant language barriers to overcome. These two translations were in high demand.

On the 9th of April, after the revelation of two security vulnerabilities over the past week, version 1.1.6.7 of the wallet client was quickly released. It was highly recommended to update as it would go a long way to increase the security and health of the network protocol. As a result of this quick update, the next major update had been delayed.

APRIL 2014

On the 10th of April at 17:18:30 UTC, user "papersheepdog" announced:

> "Direct CAD/USD <-> CGB now available on Vault of Satoshi!
>
> Please also see the Reddit post for further discussion.
> Official announcement from Vault of Satoshi.
>
> This is huge news for both the Cryptogenic Bullion Community as well as Vault of Satoshi!
>
> We encourage everyone to consider switching from their current exchange to Vault of Satoshi. Let's get some volume going! Crypto-crypto markets are also available!
>
> Stay tuned for a promotional giveaway to be announced as well as a paper outlining the evolution of the financial services industry to support the new crypto-economy!"

It was an exchange based in Canada. At this point in time, the exchange was in a state of "penetration testing". It eventually became fully operational on the 7th of October 2014. Vault of Satoshi stayed open until the 5th of January 2015 after which no further trades or deposits could be made. However, users were allowed to withdraw CBX until it fully closed its doors on the 5th of February 2015. Mike Curry, the co-founder of Vault of Satoshi, pointed out a new venture the business had shifted focus to.

On the following day, in collaboration with "CryptoSandwich" and "Bitcoin Garden", a "CGB Celebration Giveaway" went ahead to recognise the successful addition to Vault of Satoshi.

APRIL 2014

On the 21st of April at 11:03:53 UTC, user "elambert" said:

> "The 'News Beat' contest is now closed (April 21, 2014)! Thank you for the excellent entries! I would like to encourage the community to upvote their favorites this week on Reddit. The CGB team will review the entries and the feedback from the community and decide the winners early next week (week of April 28th). Great work!"

On the 27th of April at 18:34:48 UTC, user "BTCat" posted the observation:

> "CGB removed from voting on Comkort, meaning it will very soon be listed to trade.
>
> Nice job, all who voted and/or donated, Thanks.
> https://comkort.com
>
> I suggest CGB traders to send some coins to the latest exchanges to get some volume going and support buy/sell orders. If there's no volume we risk delistment.
> It may be a good opportunity for some daytrading profits, so try them out."

About one hour later, the addition to Comkort was officially announced:

> "Good News, CryptogenicBullion (CGB) was added COMKORT EXCHANGE
>
> https://comkort.com/market/trade/cgb_btc
> https://comkort.com/market/trade/cgb_ltc
> https://comkort.com/market/trade/cgb_doge
>
> GOOD LUCK & HAPPY TRADING"

Comkort opened (beta testing) on the 20th of February 2014 and went fully operational on the 1st of March 2014. It was based in Tallinn, Estonia and closed on the 20th of July 2015. This was three weeks after trading ceased to give users sufficient time to withdraw their coins (Comkort logo at the bottom of page 108).

APRIL 2014

On the 28th of April at 10:05:11 UTC, user "elambert" announced the winners of the "News Beat" contest. He said:

> "First off, thank you for the excellent entries into the competition! I certainly enjoyed this contest and hope that the participants also got a kick out of sharing their skills and knowledge. Without further ado, drum roll please............
>
> Third place (40 CGB) goes to flagin
>
> Second place (60 CGB) goes to Destro316
>
> First place (100 CGB) goes to paulmaritz!
>
> Thanks again for your participation!"

At the end of April, there were ten active exchanges (PhenixEx and OpenEx closed in 2013) on which users could trade Crypto Bullion. These were:

> Coins-e Cryptsy CoinEx Cryptokopen AllCrypt
> Bittrex Ecoinfund Swaphole PTOPEX Vault of Satoshi

Other events which occurred in the month of April were:

- On the 1st of April, user "BTCat" created a Bitcointalk thread on which he asked the community to predict the US Dollar value of one Bitcoin on the 1st of April 2015 at 00:00 UTC on the exchange called Bitstamp. Entries to the contest closed on the 1st of June 2014 after which the winner received $25 worth of CBX.

- On the 5th of April, live trading of CBX began on an exchange called PTOPEX.

- Crypto Bullion reached the top of the Comkort voting list of coin additions on the 21st of April. Six days later, live trading was initiated there.

- On the 23rd of April, user "Matheltu1" was announced as a recent addition to the core development team.

CRYPTOTOWN ON THE GROUND PROJECT
MAY 2014

I. PoW block reward halved from 0.039062 CBX to 0.019531 CBX.

II. How to celebrate the first birthday of the coin?

III. A collaborative project called "CryptoTown On The Ground" announced.

IV. Voting for Crypto Bullion on an exchange called Swisscex introduced.

V. Next wallet client was still in progress.

During the last week of April, there was not much to report on concerning the community or development team. For the first few days of May, this was no different. User "papersheepdog" encouraged people to join and participate in discussions which were being held on the official Crypto Bullion IRC Chatroom. As a result, as many people would be able to stay informed about what to expect in the future.

On the 4th of May, the PoW block reward reduced for the penultimate time:

Block #445,000 (Reward 0.039062 CBX) May 4th 2014 at 09:15:19 PM UTC

Block #445,001 (Reward 0.019531 CBX) May 4th 2014 at 09:16:32 PM UTC

MAY 2014

On the 5th of May, people were concerned why the value of the coin was not reflecting the recent effort being put in by the development team and community as a whole. On the same day at 10:11:41 UTC, user "elambert" gave his own personal opinion on why this was the case. He was quoted as saying:

> "Tough to say... However, work continues
>
> We will be launching some exciting new marketing campaigns in the next couple of weeks to aid in CGB's exposure and will have an update on the new client (major overhaul) in the coming weeks. May is shaping up to be an exciting month and we will continue to build on the established groundwork throughout June leading up to a celebration of CGB's first birthday on June 27th! We have less than 8 weeks until the birthday bash and lots of fun planned so grab a seat and join in!"

On the following day, user "elambert" asked members of community for ideas on how to celebrate the first birthday. A couple of suggestions put forward were:

- A "Google Hangout" video chat between core development team members.

- A competition to see how many individuals or businesses one can introduce to cryptocurrency. One would have to demonstrate how to install the wallet client as well as send/receive coins. This would run from the 27th of May for exactly one month.

By inviting as many people as possible to engage in this celebration, a greater awareness of Crypto Bullion was sought after. User "papersheepdog" knew the importance of broadening the discussion on Facebook, Reddit and Twitter.

One week later on the 14th of May at 21:06:38 UTC, user "papersheepdog" said:

> "There has been a lot of interesting discussion on Reddit about getting CGB into the hands of communities through local interaction and a holistic multi-service approach. Community involvement is needed, ask the tough questions, get involved! We encourage you all to participate."

On the 26th of May, a collaborative project between the community and the IndiaMikeZulu Organisation was announced by user "papersheepdog". Known as "CryptoTown On The Ground", and open to all cryptocurrency enthusiasts, its main purpose was to facilitate the spread of cryptocurrencies through face-to-face, human being contact. Many details at this time were yet to be confirmed.

> "The project aims to provide guidelines and resources for structuring your own CryptoTown Neighborhood, enrolling your business, or participating as a community member. This project is founded on the principles of self-sufficiency, decentralization and sustainability."

On the following day, an exchange called Swisscex introduced Crypto Bullion to their voting list of potential coin additions at https://www.swisscex.com/voting. Registered users were now able to vote for CBX three times per hour. However, user "dygus" was not enthused about the prospect of the coin becoming active on another exchange. He was quoted as saying:

> "We don't need another exchange we need investors, a bit pump. We are already on bittrex which has big trading volume. If ppl will see this coin with bigger trading volume, than they will start to read about CGB and spread the word."

As announced in a weekly team update on the penultimate day of May, efforts were still being made to create the next wallet client. It was expected to be released in the next couple of weeks depending on how successful testing went.

On the last day of the month at 21:11:28 UTC, user "elambert" created a Bitcointalk thread titled "Happy Birthday CGB!!!!!!!!!!!!!". He introduced the thread by saying:

> "Ok guys and gals, I am kicking off this thread to lead up to the first birthday of Cryptogenic Bullion on June 27th! We have a number of amazing developments (some public, some private) that will be revealed as the month of June progresses. All the while I will be running some giveaways and contests on this thread."

Crypto Bullion—History of the First Year

ONE YEAR ANNIVERSARY OF CRYPTO BULLION
JUNE 2014

I. Responsibilities of lead developer "artiface" scaled back.

II. Efforts made to expand the Core CBX Development Team.

III. No block reward reduction at block number 495,001.

IV. Donations to a new marketing campaign encouraged.

V. Last block of the first year existence of the blockchain timestamped.

Despite the dedication shown by the core development team and wider community, the market capitalisation was slowly decreasing. On the 2nd of June, it had decreased slightly below $200,000. As the Director of Marketing and Strategy, user "papersheepdog" was still enthusiastic and he was still contributing greatly to build up the community. He was quoted as saying:

> "I suggest we move forward without weighing the price as such an important indicator. Again, It has no effect on the effort that the CGB Core Team and community is putting up."

Besides this, lead developer user "artiface" had recently been overwhelmed with a personal family emergency. Consequently, he asked for his responsibilities to be scaled back temporarily. The next wallet client release date was now uncertain.

JUNE 2014

On the 4th of June, user "papersheepdog" said the following:

> "It seems that the altcoin world is really grinding through a tough patch as Bitcoin recovers from the recent hostile positions taken against it by government and big business alike. For CGB, it is a bit of a unique situation. Very few coins have had to deal with the turbulence of moving beyond the mining phase, which seems to attract all of the attention. We now have to forge ahead and create value in ways other than mining focused speculation. Up until this point, CGB has been tracing along its original vision, and will continue to justify the demand for an asset made to act like gold or silver as well as a cryptocurrency could. This is a great premise for a currency, but the details are still not widely known as to how this is so and why it matters. As we continue toward our educational objectives, we are also undertaking a major course change for the CGB community which aims to create real world value for not only CGB, but all deserving cryptocurrencies."

Efforts were also being made to expand the Crypto Bullion Development Team. As part of the "CryptoTown On The Ground" project, the objective was to appeal and an engage with the wider cryptocurrency community and beyond. Talented individuals who were willing to help Crypto Bullion move forward were encouraged to come forward by sending a private message to either user "elambert" or user "papersheepdog".

On the 5th of June at 00:41:00 UTC, the top three cryptocurrencies in terms of market capitalisation were:

1	Bitcoin	$ 8,253,392,940	$ 641.94	12,857,025 BTC	$ 37,707,282	-2.89 %
2	Litecoin	$ 319,425,329	$ 11.02	28,992,504 LTC	$ 4,065,819	-3.69 %
3	Nxt	$ 75,359,537	$ 0.075360	999,997,096 NXT*	$ 678,830	+10.53 %

There was no proof of work block reward halving at block number 495,001. The last reduction would take place later at block number 545,001 to 0.1 CBX on the 13th of July 2014.

Block #495,001 (Reward 0.019531 CBX) June 8th 2014 at 10:17:35 PM UTC

On the 18th of June, user "VonSpass", the current Marketing Strategy Director, joined a discussion about the topic of inflation. There were concerns that annual ROI provided by proof of stake was not attracting new members to the community. He did not recommend a stark increase in the annual inflation, but said:

> "I think, an acceptance has to be made that CGB is not yet failed, but is failing. If we keep things the same way, it will fail; so let's accept the fact that things have to change for success to happen."

On the 18th of June at 18:56:29 UTC, user "Killiz" said:

> "What we need is a renewed vibrance within the community. The one thing CGB is lacking is an active community. An active community is the strength of any particular coin.
>
> The miners have left the scene, but what do the majority of miners do? They sell. What we need to do is to educate these miners, who are knowingly mining a longterm worthless coin, only because it is profitable at that moment in time, to put some of their profits into CGB as an investment.
>
> The POS reward mustn't be increased above 2%, I agree with myself and PSD about that. It should be looked at as merely a POS security which only adds 2% max inflation, nothing more. Less is more!
>
> I keep reading how CGB needs more services. Do holders of physical bullion demand this? CGB is digital bullion, and should be treated as such. Simply a store of wealth, to be exchanged for a more widely accepted currency as and when needed in the future."

User "papersheepdog" was glad a constructive discussion about the long term metrics of the coin was being held. He was quoted as saying:

> "We have plenty of room to expand into the economy of course; cryptocurrencies are hardly known and yet badly needed. This expansion is exactly what the CryptoTown project is about. Creating new facets of the economy for CGB to be held in, new demand created through consultancy and advocacy."

JUNE 2014

Furthermore, user "VonSpass" emphasised the importance of Crypto Bullion adapting in order to successfully move forward. He thought the initiatives such as the campaigns on Reddit, the newly redesigned official website and the weekly updates did not have the desired effect of properly promoting Crypto Bullion. He recommended the following:

1. Make it possible for people to buy/sell goods/services solely with CBX.
2. Create online games which require CBX as the only form of payment.
3. Change the coin specification to bring miners back on board.

On the 19th of June at 00:44:50 UTC, user "elambert" said:

> "Guys, absolutely love the debate and idea sharing here! My opinion, we should stay true to our initial mission, values and code. I just had a look at coinmarketcap, you know that 3 of the top 10 market cap coins are not mineable - at all?
>
> I agree there is a place for highly inflationary coins, but there is also a place for the stable low inflation niche that CGB is creating. CGB was one of the first PoS coins, one of the first to implement the accelerated subsidy halving, one of the first to move to PoS as a higher payout than PoW. All coins (even Bitcoin) will at some point in their life cycle come to a cross road where they have to either move away from appeasing miners or change their code and word to their earlier adopters. We are just a trend setter here again.
>
> CGB has, and in my opinion should continue to logically envision the path ahead and move proactively rather than in a reactionary manner."

There were people who agreed with user "elambert" that the current specification should not be changed. They thought the original vision of Crypto Bullion as a rare crypto commodity would yield results in the long term. It was this characteristic that had attracted investors to the coin in the first place. As a means to move forward, an greater investment from interested parties, a higher trading volume on exchanges and an expanding public awareness strategy were highlighted aims.

JUNE 2014

On the 24th of June, the last "CGB Core Team Weekly Update" was released as a brief update. Preparations were still being made for the coin's first birthday on the 27th of June 2014. A big favour was asked of the community:

> "We need donations. We are struggling to put together the funds for an ambitious professional marketing campaign. By next month, many of you will be shocked at the quality and exposure of our next big piece. For the ability to continue to fully capture the momentum we will need real funding. CGB is ready, CryptoTown is the face of the next big push. Your contributions could mean the difference between kicking off the party and waiting around for something to happen. This is a special appeal to anyone who may have the ability; don't just hold CGB, invest in it (CGB Foundation).
>
> Details on Friday's party may be divulged shortly."

In less than twenty four hours, user "IMZ" was the first to publicly donate 100 CBX to the marketing campaign. On the 25th of June at 22:44:41 UTC, user "elambert" was grateful for the support and expanded on why funding would help:

> "As PSD mentioned, we are in the works of putting together a professional marketing campaign that will expose CGB to an audience that reaches far beyond the day-traders and miners that make up the majority of BCT. The only issue is that this is very costly. Donations are encouraged and welcomed! If you have a stake in CGB, please help us and lets do this as a community."

On the 27th of June, the last block of the first year existence of the CBX blockchain was timestamped. A total of 952,106.80947519 CBX had been generated:

Block #521,987 (Reward 0.019531 CBX) June 27th 2014 at 05:43:32 PM UTC

On the following day, the blockchain had been publicly available for one year:

Block #522,482 (Reward 0.019531 CBX) June 28th 2014 at 01:56:59 AM UTC

APPENDIX

APPENDIX

ARTICLE ONE

"The Rare, Interest Bearing, Bitcoin Alternative—Cryptogenic Bullion"

10th of September 2013

The Rare, Interest Bearing, Bitcoin Alternative—Cryptogenic Bullion

September 10, 2013

"NEW YORK—(ACCESSWIRE—September 10th, 2013) / MarketerMedia /— The number of professional online services incorporating Cryptogenic Bullion is growing at a rapid rate and the currency is currently trading for approximately 500 CGB per 1 BTC. A fork of the virtual currency Novacoin, Cryptogenic Bullion is desgned to be rare, interest baring, peer-to-eer virtual commodity with the same decentralised characteristics of Bitcoin but with some key differences. Cryptogenic Bullion's innovations include an accelerated decrease of the mining subsidy, almost immediate transaction time and 2% annual interest eligible for Bullion that has been stationary in a user's wallet for at least 30 days. Cryptogenic Bullion has been well received in the digital currency ecosystem. The official Facebook page has over 4,500 fans, and the official CGB website has been translated into Dutch and Chinese.

The team behind Cryptogenic Bullion is comprised of digital currency enthusiasts with many years of experience in the Bitcoin ecosystem and beyond; having spent many years mining, programming and working on Internet technology projects. Unique among alternative cryptocurrency teams, CGB also has many years of experience in business management and marketing, ensuring CGB carves out a significant niche for itself in the digitalcurrency ecosystem. Much like Staoshi Nakamoto of Bitcoin, the lead developer of CGB has remained anonymous—but the anonymous developer tackles problems and maintains the integiry of the CGB protocol. This is extremely important for the longevity of the project. Elambert, the founder of Cryptogenic Bullion, is a married man with an 8-month-old son who both works as a data analyst and is also extensively involved in other online businesses and pursuits. Managing the marketing and project development aspects of CGB is Mercury Stills, an entrepreneur with a passion of emerging technologies who founded his first company in the year 2000.

Team CGB is currently pursuing an aggressive marketing campaign via social networking sites like Facebook, GooglePlus, Twitter, LinkedIn, Sina, Baidu, Sohu and more. Moreover, Team CGB will initiate a billboard campaign across Europe, starting in Nicosia, Cyprus later this year. The more people who are aware of Cryptogenic Bullion and the financial and business innovation provided by virtual commodities and virtual currencies, the more people will embrace the unprecedented possibilities inherent to the emerging disruptive technology of global digital currencies. In this way Cryptogenic Bullion's extensive marketing not only benefits the CGB project but the entire cryptocurrency space itself.

The Winklevoss twin's intention to offer the world's first Bitcoin exchange-traded fund (ETF) could be the precursor to a diverse range of alternative virtual currency ETFs. As an interest bearing, relatively rare, virtual commodity, Cryptogenic Bullion will be perfectly positioned to attract fund manager's capital, which will generate massive potential for large long-term increases in value. Team CGB is currently reaching out to investors and business owners who may want to diversify some of their BTC holdings into CGB to potentially remedy price volatility. Any individual who contacts team CGB to incorporate Cryptogenic Bullion into their business processes will be warmly received.

With the professionalism and vision of the Cryptogenic Bullion core team, this digital commodity is operating in a different paradigm to the majority of alternative cryptocurrencies. The CGB protocol's primary innovations of a 2% annual interest rate, and its relative rarity and fatser transaction time as opposed to Bitcoin also bode well for the digital currency's future. A diverse ecosystem is a healthy one, and due to its unique properties Cryptogenic Bullion may well become one of the cryptocurrencies of choice in the emerging digital currency investment space.

Visit http://cryptogenicbullion.org/ for more information."

ARTICLE TWO

"Cryptogenic Bullion—The Virtual Commodity Blurring the Lines Between Currency and Big Data"

18th of November 2013

Cryptogenic Bulliob—The Virtual Commodity Blurring the Lines Between Currency and Big Data

November 18, 2013

"The lead project developer of Cryptogenic Bullion (CB), Mercury Stills, recently unveiled details of his major project, MADEsparq Project. A white paper has been published on the CB website. From the white paper, "This new paradigm, named the MADEsparq Project, aims to blur the defining lines between currency, technology, and data by using the CB block chain to mediate the mapping of data to create, and add value, to content and unstructured and semi-structured data."

The MADEsparq Project website, MADEsparq.org, is under construction but will begin to offer some of the functionality mentioned in the white paper by mid-January. Moreover, the client software will have an open alpha release by the middle of next month. "The project is meant to intricately involve the inherent random structure of the Cryptogenic Bullion block chain and spark new ways of categorising and collaborating about data, regardless of your interest or level of expertise. It's an open-source, open-collaboration project, so it made sense to have the alpha release be open as well," said Stills.

It's that intricate relationship between CB and the growing number of participants using the CB network and block chain (ie. The public ledger system similar to Bitcoin) to mediate all the data categorizations and mappings, from a variety of knowledge-domains, that creates intrinsic value for the virtual commodity. "I honestly think this paradigm I'm trying to create will change everyone's perspective on the possibilities of virtual currencies. We can do so much with them, not just as a form of transferring value. And that, in turn, will help accelerate mass adoption of CB and Bitcoin."

The MADEsparq Project supports only the virtual commodity, Cryptogenic Bullion. But other virtual currencies and commodities might be supported. "Eventually, Bitcoin will be supported, but not until we're in beta development."

Cryptogenic Bullion's price at the time of this writing is about 0.0017 per Bitcoin or $0.92 and trades on various virtual currency exchanges, and its total market value is about $900K, which is miniscule compared to Bitcoin's $7 billion market value. "Cryptogenic Bullion was released less than five months ago and we're just now announcing our first major project. It's obviously an amazing time for participants to get a stake in the currency and to try to be independent from the corporate banking sector, while also pursuing one's own dreams. There's dozens of global currencies backed by centralized and often corrupt governments. Now, the people are taking all finance matters into their own hands. Soon there will be a vast system of virtual currencies and commodities, many with their own niche, akin to our current global system of fiat currencies. Decentralized, peer-to-peer virtual currency networks will change the way the world works for the better.""

For more information about Cryptogenic Bullion visit http://cryptogenicbullion.org/.

Contact Info:
Name: Mercury Stills
Email: info@CryptogenicBullion.org

www.ingramcontent.com/pod-product-compliance
Lightning Source LLC
Chambersburg PA
CBHW070322190526
45169CB00005B/1711